Vanessa L. Oc... *an's Journey into* .... extensively on children and families for *Woman's Day, Child, Newsday,* and numerous other publications. A recipient of a fellowship in creative writing from the National Endowment for the Arts, she teaches both religion and writing at Drew University and is currently a Dorot Fellow at CLAL, the National Jewish Center for Learning and Leadership.

SAFE
AND
SOUND

Protecting Your Child in
an Unpredictable World

Vanessa L. Ochs

Penguin Books

For Mims and Bernside

PENGUIN BOOKS
Published by the Penguin Group
Penguin Books USA Inc., 375 Hudson Street,
New York, New York 10014, U.S.A.
Penguin Books Ltd, 27 Wrights Lane,
London W8 5TZ, England
Penguin Books Australia Ltd, Ringwood,
Victoria, Australia
Penguin Books Canada Ltd, 10 Alcorn Avenue,
Toronto, Ontario, Canada M4V 3B2
Penguin Books (N.Z.) Ltd, 182–190 Wairau Road,
Auckland 10, New Zealand

Penguin Books Ltd, Registered Offices:
Harmondsworth, Middlesex, England

First published in Penguin Books 1995

1 3 5 7 9 10 8 6 4 2

The Zuni prayer on page 196 is from *Zuni Ritual Poetry* by Ruth Bunzel, Forty-
seventh Annual Report, Bureau of American Ethnology, Washington, D.C.,
1929–30, 1932.

LIBRARY OF CONGRESS CATALOGING IN PUBLICATION DATA
Ochs, Vanessa L.
Safe and sound: protecting your child in an unpredictable world/
Vanessa L. Ochs.
p.   cm.
Includes bibliographical references.
ISBN 0 14 01.17880 5
1. Safety education.   2. Children's accidents—Prevention.
3. Child rearing.   I. Title.
HQ770.7.O26   1995
649'.1—dc20   94–45521

Printed in the United States of America
Set in Adobe Centaur
Designed by Virginia Norey

Acknowledgments

Research for this book was funded, in part, by an NEA Fellowship in Creative Writing.

I am grateful for the assistance I received from Pamela Klassen, Rose Weinheimer, Juliana Ochs, and Elizabeth Ochs, and I thank my colleagues and students at Drew University who listened to my thoughts on overprotection and responded generously out of the depths of their own experiences. To all those parents, children, and parents-to-be who allowed themselves to be interviewed, I can only hope that this has become the book they'd hoped it would be. For their psychological expertise I thank Barbara Hyatt Pressley and Drs. Guita Epstein, Michelle Friedman, and Roger Granet.

My thanks go to Mindy Werner at Penguin, who recognized that protecting children appropriately in a dangerous world is an overwhelming issue for parents. And finally, my thanks go, as always, to Molly Friedrich.

Contents

Preface

I became intensely overprotective shortly after I was injured in an automobile accident. My children, then seven and eleven, were not even with me but were safe at school. Until then, as far as I knew, I gave overprotection little thought. Of course, I thought about plain, garden-variety protection. This was the bedrock of my mothering; my waking hours were consumed by protective activities. I prepared wholesome meals, watched for strep, kept inoculations up to date. I taught the girls to guard their self-esteem and cautioned them not to take things other people said too seriously. I protected them from my own stresses ("No, honey, I'm not angry at you. I'm just going nuts: I have to finish an article, grade twenty term papers, and get you the black camisole leotard at Capezio's."). I spent hours listening to what the girls were saying and listened hard, as parents do, for what they were not saying. I taught them to protect themselves by keeping their eyes open for danger, idiocy, and malevolence. The right balances were in position: The kids were watched but were not put under surveillance; they were loved, but not smothered.

My husband, Peter, had been my partner in these activities all along, redoubling or complementing my own protective efforts. He's the parent who made sure the kids got enough exercise, who reminded them to bring water bottles on hikes. He's the one who worried about a kid's loneliness or sadness and acted upon it creatively, instead of hoping it would pass.

At the same time, we both tried to foster freedom. When our girls were very young, we wanted them to be free to discover how to use their bodies for moving, manipulating and discovering the little worlds around them, even if that meant getting scratches and bumps. As they got older, we hoped they could freely choose the activities, play materials, and friends that gave them pleasure. As well as we could, we encouraged them to express their emotions.

If I compared myself to different kinds of parents I knew —the ones I'd categorize as negligent, permissive, particularly cautious and concerned, or extremely overprotective—I placed myself somewhere in the middle. I had been wildly overprotected as a child, so I had made a point of raising my children with looseness, calm, and measure and not making their lives or my own miserable with fear. When people would notice my behavior and say to me "You never freak out with your kids" or "You never raise your voice," I took those as compliments, signs that my protective approach was working. Early on I bent over backward to be optimistic and slow to panic, and over the years this became habitual. When one daughter came home from a school camping trip with her tiny face red and swollen from poison ivy, I heard myself saying, "Well now, let's get you fixed up." I appeared, to myself and others, to have effectively fashioned myself into someone who kissed boo-boos away, someone who imagined a child's problems would be worked out one way or another.

My method was simply to use the lesson of opposites: What my parents had done in raising me, I did otherwise. If vestiges of the ancestral hysteria welled up in me, I repressed them. My "oppose and repress" method seemed to work. True, I had never sent either child off to sleep-away camp, but I allowed them to have lives.

The car accident—a rear-end collision that left me with serious whiplash and related injuries—had a curious effect on me. Beyond the physical injury, I was not the same. The calm I experienced immediately after the accident was eventually replaced with panic. I found myself in a state of hypervigilance, a fairly common delayed response to trauma, particularly among those who, at first, appear to be so utterly together that they have emerged from the trauma emotionally unscathed, as if nothing out of the ordinary had happened.

But I had lost all illusion of safety. I believed that if I could not keep harm from myself, I was all the more powerless to keep truly awful things from befalling my girls. The reverberations of my accident went beyond my own body. The accident had endangered my daughters, a glitch in the universe had been created, a hole through which evil, misfortune, and danger would leak.

My immediate response was to overprotect.

In order to make it through the day, it helps if we believe that bad things will probably not happen to us, particularly if we take precautions, act wisely, and keep our eyes open. While we recognize that "bad things happen to good people," we trust that we will be among the good people who squeak by. We can fly because we believe our plane won't crash and our airport won't be bombed by terrorists. We can put our child on the school bus each morning because we trust their driver won't be the drunk one who steers the bus over a ravine. To go forward each day, we block out most of the bad things that could go wrong.

If we couldn't do that, if we couldn't install that shield against fear, how ever could we step into planes, buses, cars, elevators, streets—anything that entailed risk? We'd never allow our children to leave our arms.

Had I been able to pin blame for the accident on myself, perhaps I would have moved on more speedily with my life. Had I been able to say, "I'll never go through a yellow light again," then I might have felt I would be safe in the future; I would have felt that I had some leverage.

But I was not to blame, and there was no yellow light. A car crashed into my friend Charlotte's car as we waited patiently in the proper lane, signaling correctly to make a left turn.

I couldn't bear the feeling of having lost control; I became furious and frightened. A new logic took over my thinking, and there was no willing it away with little pep talks to myself and attempts at being rational. If things went terribly wrong once, I reasoned, they would in all likelihood go wrong again and yet again, because I had no control over evil—regarding myself or my children.

My friend Doreen commiserated with me, and though she didn't make me more safe or less crazy, she did make me feel less alone. When she had lost a baby in infancy, Doreen said, she had also lost her sense of invulnerability ("Before, I always felt my husband and I and our little boys had this perfectly charmed life. It was as though a lucky star shined over us"). If once they had been safe on the periphery, after the baby died they had finally gotten noticed in the scheme of things. They were open targets, their safety up for grabs. Having lost control that one time, Doreen felt they would always be vulnerable. Now she takes nothing for granted. When Doreen flies with her family or drives with them to Grandma's house, she never blithely assumes they will get there safely. Walking outside at night, watching the fierce wind blow through the trees, Doreen looks at her neighbors' homes and cars parked in their driveways. How frail our attempts to protect our families are, she thinks, even with all the Sheetrock and metal in the world. "Life is tenuous," Doreen says. "We hang on a string."

There is, I have often thought, something to be said for going through life in a state of stunned gratitude. The goal of so many spiritual disciplines is to become extremely aware of how tenuous and temporal happiness is. While a state of mind that links gratitude and fragility can work nicely if we meditate in an ashram or shear sheep in a monastery, it doesn't play well if we drive kids in carpools. Like most parents, I had depended upon my shield against fear just to get by each day. I liked taking it for granted that the furnace wouldn't explode before I finished scrambling the eggs for breakfast. I liked cruising the aisles of Foodtown without thinking about salmonella and botulism.

Having lost my shield against fear, I planned my days assuming the worst and attempting to avoid it. My own children seemed terribly at risk, but so did all children. I would see a school bus on the road and cry. I could not look at children without imagining their parents standing empty-armed, mourning their loss.

My husband took Julie, my older daughter, to a water park, where they planned to go down the water slides as they had done before. Traditionally I never went along, since I do not enjoy such amusements myself, but I never stayed home worrying either: If the amusements weren't safe and regularly inspected by some federal agency, the park would be out of business, right?

That day, I had convinced myself that Peter and Julie would decide to try out the park's newest attraction, one I had seen advertised on television: the bungee jump. I pictured them flying off the high tower, the bungee cords snapping. I kept vigil by my front window all that day and into the night, waiting to see the headlights of their car. I couldn't read or eat. I just sat there imagining the sound of ambulances.

They strolled through the door at nine at night, having stopped for Mexican food on the way home. They said the bungee jump, which hadn't even opened yet, would never have interested them. "Why did you think we'd do that?" Julie asked, showing me a scrape she had gotten on her foot from the rough bottom of the wave pool. As I covered her scrape with Bacitracin, so eager to spread on some kind of protective shield, I celebrated the abrasion, the small pain she endured that substituted for a larger pain that had been averted.

We had made it through that day but were still at risk. "Oh my God," I said to myself each time Peter drove off with the girls in the convertible, "everything that's precious to me is contained in that vulnerable contraption." My vigil would begin all over again. What was safe and what was unsafe? The world was just too dangerous and the potential for catastrophe was everywhere. A wave could pull them under, a skyscraper could topple over on them, the dishwasher could explode. I'd stare at the crack in the ceiling caused by a leak in the roof and picture the house caving in as we slept. Something bad had happened once, and it could happen again. If I couldn't keep myself from harm, would my children, so vulnerable and fragile, be spared? I looked around me and noticed that I was not the only parent who was almost too swamped with fear to make it through the day.

I kept the children around me like nestlings. Having written about child development and family life for years, I knew I was overprotecting the girls, and I was well aware of the tremendous disservice I was doing them. I was curtailing their lives, forbidding them from taking risks and leaping freely into life, feeding them my own fears. Still, months went by before I could contain my anxiety. More time passed before I could stop overprotecting, and even more time before I could let my daughters go.

How awful for a parent to bind up a child, physically and emotionally, and here I was, doing it to my own girls. I was practicing the kind of child-rearing I had sworn I would never be guilty of ever since the days my teenage buddies and I would intone *The Prophet*, by Khalil Gibran. On the scales of wise and deep, we thought nothing matched what Gibran had to say about children. We were all rebelling against our parents, the "establishment," who worried we would become free, unfettered "flower children." We particularly liked Gibran's notion that we were *not* our parents' children but, rather, children of Life; that we came from our parents but didn't belong to them.

We adored Gibran's image: Parents are the bow from which "living arrows are set forth." Couldn't our parents understand how much we yearned to be arrows shot from their steady, directing bow so we could fly, soar, be free? Didn't they remember what it was like to be young? If Mr. Gibran were our father, we would never have to bristle with his interference. What we would have done with the freedom if it were granted to us, we did not know, but I gather we would have kept up with our homework, learned vocabulary words for the S.A.T.s, and showered regularly. We just wanted to know what freedom felt like. I vowed never to forget what it was like to be a teenager yearning for freedom. And I didn't forget. But it would become impossible for me to release my own children from my bow.

While I recovered from my neck and back injuries in the months following the accident, scribbling in a journal because I couldn't yet sit at my computer and work, I tried to write my way out of my state of fearfulness so that I could stop overprotecting. In this process of healing, I found myself re-discovering my own overprotected childhood. The memories surfaced and splashed over me with such intensity. At first, even though it now seems so obvious, I couldn't trace the connection between this aspect of my childhood and my cur-rent situation. I knew I had been profoundly overprotected, treated as a catastrophe-and-sickness-prone child, too vulner-able to survive a "cootie"-filled world; but while this once angered and saddened me, I had ceased to reflect on it much from the moment I married at twenty (not a moment too soon!) and felt legally and emotionally beyond my parents' clutches. I had escaped that part of my past and moved on.

Or so I thought.

I recorded this flood of memories from my overprotected childhood, filling one pad after another. In time, I would dis-cover that my accident wasn't the only reason I had been opened to full-scale panic and given to hypervigilance in re-spect to myself and my daughters. The panic was surely a belated effect of having once been so tightly held, so rigidly shielded. Overprotected.

If overprotection had once made me feel rage, and I had

swallowed it, in my current state I could contain it no longer. I needed to acknowledge how angry I was that the overprotection had stifled, limited, and humiliated me; I needed to confront all the sadness, the curtailment of self, and the feelings of ineptitude.

How fearful my mother was for me and my sister, Susan, seven years younger than I. My mother was major general of fear; and my stepfather carried out her instructions to curtail her hysteria.

One day, by mistake, he taught me to swim in the Atlantic Ocean. Deep, deep water over my head! It was terrifying, exciting, the first and only wild thing I had ever done. Whales, sharks, killer jelly fish, the "undertoad"—who knew what was out there? Once the urge to vomit passed, I experienced a feeling totally foreign to me: thrill. And I rather liked it. With my stepfather holding me, I floated on my back, and when he gradually pulled away his arms, there I was, buoyant in a sunny, wet universe. When my fingers got too prunelike and we emerged from the water together, my mother (who, like her siblings and her parents, had never learned to swim) threatened my stepfather in front of all Brighton Beach: "I will leave you! The child's lips are blue. You have endangered her life!"

Showing remorse, though he seemed unsure of his crime, my stepfather bundled me in towels and blankets and poured me my first cup of hot, sweet coffee from our thermos bottle. It was delicious. My mother shook her head. "Now you have stunted her growth," she said, dismayed that he had absolutely no instinct for a child's survival. That was the end of beach swimming. The next time we went to the beach, I taught myself to knit and made a shawl for my Barbie.

Our parents never feared we would turn to drugs or alcohol or fall in with a bad crowd or fall off the seat of a wild boy's motorcycle. We, Susan and I, were nice, quiet girls who came from a good family in the bosom of the suburbs. Such dangers that befell other people's children were unthinkable for us, as impossible as a volcano erupting over Long Island. Our parents never feared we would break our legs skiing, be thrown horseback riding, or drown while rowing a boat. Such forbidden activities—add to the list ice-skating, roller-skating, and climbing on monkey bars—were, I assumed, for daredevils and maniacs: the kind of people who earned a living diving on horseback into pools in Atlantic City. We had heard that a cousin of ours rode a horse, which I found hard to believe. All of our relatives were the "fragile" children of fearful parents. The cousin's horse turned out to be a depressed, rope-led pony at a county fair.

For indoor amusement, I read piles of difficult books, and Susan composed on the piano. At least we were not overprotected from sedentary intellectual and creative challenges. We sang, too, and read Shakespeare's plays with Southern accents, and we could giggle, as long as we didn't get too "worked up." Beyond that, I recall being permitted to exercise along with the first half of Jack La Lanne's TV show. After that I'd be told, "It's too much for you. You're too thin already and you're sweating." Sweating was a huge source of fear. If the backs of our necks were warm and damp when our mother thrust her hand down our collars, we would be admonished—"You're sweating!" or, as if we were cars in summer traffic jams, "You've overheated!" What was the crime of sweating? Were we at fault for having performed the activity that lead to the sweat (too much rope jumping, getting worked up over the fancies in jacks)? Was our mistake having let down our guard enough to slip into the precarious state of being heated up? Scolded for a crime we could neither understand nor control, we would sulk off to our rooms, feeling both guilty and innocent.

For outdoor exercise, called "getting air," we could sit on a beach chair in a sunny spot in the back yard holding sun reflectors up to our faces, for she believed that the more sun we got, the healthier we would be. We could play jacks on the porch if we sat on a cushion to prevent chills or splinters in our bottoms, we could bounce a pink ball for "*A* my name is Alice," or we could walk down the block to the Peninsula Public Library's bookmobile. Winters, if the snowy day was sufficiently sunny, we pulled each other around in the yard in a plastic boat that looked like a baby's bathtub. We couldn't do this for too long, however: Dressed as we were in long underwear, sweaters, and snowsuits, we quickly overheated and grew faint in the white glare of sun reflecting from the snow. When that happened, we were rushed indoors to tuck our heads between our knees until we came to. After having regained consciousness, we had to run our fingers under luke-warm water to ward off frostbite.

While all the other children waited in front of the Sunday school building to be picked up by their carpools, we had to wait indoors, as the fumes of cars and buses going down West Broadway would asphyxiate us. I felt so stupid standing inside the doorway. What were the other children thinking? I prayed that they might conclude that it was my parents who were nuts, and not I.

My mother wanted to ask our pediatrician to write a note excusing us from gym to protect us from bodily harm and overexertion. We begged her not to and, to our surprise, won. She muttered "Stubborn . . . stubborn," suggesting that not only would we pay for the harm we'd encounter in gym, but that she was the one who would pay tenfold, with mad dashes to the orthopedist who would set our fingers in metal splints. (She was right; every volleyball season, she rushed us to the orthopedist and I came home with another finger in a metal splint.) As for swimming in high school, we had no say: She made the pediatrician write a note inventing chronic ear problems that ruled out the activity. We didn't even try begging: There was no way we'd be permitted to leave the swimming pool with wet hair and enter the cold school hallways and "catch a chill and get pneumonia." I didn't mind. After the day my stepfather had gotten into so much trouble for teaching me to swim at Brighton Beach, I hated swimming.

One day, when my sister's friend was out riding his bike, he was knifed and killed. In response to this boy's violent and senseless death, my mother fell to pieces. She always knew how limited a parent's protection was, but now all protection seemed a meaningless gesture. My recollection is that she took to her room for weeks, eating in bed, and came out only when she was ready to overprotect again.

In the short run, we were indeed protected from harm. We, who never skied, never broke our legs skiing. Having never owned tennis rackets, we never sprained our ankles on the tennis court. But in the long run, there are too many things I simply cannot do now and cannot imagine I could ever learn (skiing, playing tennis, roller-skating); and there are the things I can do only after overcoming enormous doubt and trepidation (driving in any city other than my own, traveling roads I don't know, flying to a strange destination and getting around). Before I go off on a journey, I must picture every aspect of it over and over again so that when the journey actually takes place, I have the illusion that I have already been there. I had thought this plague of doubt and trepidation was just a quirk of personality, but surely it was the residue of overprotection.

Early on, I protested the overprotection, complaining that compared to other children, I could never do anything or go anywhere. This got me into big trouble. My ingratitude threw my mother into spells of tears. "I will not forget this day as long as I live! Is this just?" she cried as she lay on her bed, exhausted from virtuous worry. "The children of bad mothers kiss their feet."

By bad mothers, she meant those who let their children go to birthday parties even when they had sniffles. I yearned, even for one day, to be the child of a "bad" mother. What a fling: I would go hatless, sockless, undershirtless, eat Franco-American Spaghetti-O's from a can. Susan and I may have been sheltered, but we were not idiots. We could distinguish the "bad" mothers as well as the "bad" fathers from the truly neglectful ones who didn't care. The "bad" parents we craved had a hold on reality: They believed their kids could make it through the day without breaking down, and they believed they themselves were adequate to the difficult, but not hellish, task of raising kids.

Later, as a teenager, I learned to lie very well, and in this way I didn't miss out on everything that was fun. What I couldn't get permission to do, I did on the sly. If my mother asked, "Did you stand next to a nun on the Long Island Railroad like I told you?" and there had been no nuns in sight, I, recalling the Madeleine books, made up a convent on an outing. As I got older, the lies got bigger, better, more frequent. A former boyfriend recently told me, "I'll never forget that your parents let you do anything." In truth, at a certain point, my parents simply had no idea what I was actually doing. Not that I hitched cross-country or took up with a commune—I snuck off with girlfriends to see the seals at the Central Park Zoo and then took the subway downtown to see the movie *Funny Girl.* For such lies, I never felt guilty; I just didn't want to be caught and have to hear all the screaming and crying. By lying, I looked out for myself, circumvented some of the overprotection, and granted myself a more normal life and more challenging, maturing experiences than I would otherwise have had.

My mother would constantly advise Susan and me, "Don't have children. Repeat aloud after me: Don't have children." Such bizarre advice to give children. We knew it then, even as we repeated the words aloud. We were a horrible burden that my mother didn't feel adequate to handle, but could we have been the headache she experienced us to be? We heard the advice (was it a threat, a command?) and were made to repeat it every time we were driven to doctors.

We knew we were well-loved children, and we knew the

love was strong and constant, but we also knew it was being expressed in a way that made us miserable. My mother did not mean to say she regretted having Susan and me. We were aware of that, for we were her life, valued high above any canvas she had ever painted or room she had rendered dust-free. If she worried about us with the fullness of her heart, she marvelled at us and rooted for us with a heart equally full. Advising us not to have children was yet another gesture of overprotection; this was how she warned us that a parent's worry was too overwhelming to bear. It was her way of saying that a parent can come to resent children for causing so much love and, consequently, so much anxiety to well up. This was her ultimate gesture of protection, to protect us from having children over whom we'd worry ourselves sick.

I ignored her advice. Susan eventually would, too, and now has two little boys. I had trusted that if I were to have children, I could raise them differently, without overprotecting.

For a while, my plan worked. And then it stopped.

PART
ONE

1

Overprotection

The experiencing of frustrations, disappointments, loss of what is loved . . . forms a significant part of the child's upbringing, and surely, a most important aim of education should be to enable the child to manage life unaided.

—D. W. Winnicott

I have written this book for parents who recognize that children are fragile and vulnerable in body and spirit. It is for parents who have been tempted to respond to the terror and brokenness of the world we live in by overprotecting their children, either sometimes or often, either a little or a great deal. It is for parents who are surprised to find themselves overprotecting at all, and who are trying, as I am, to figure out how to protect their children reasonably and responsibly, and to let them go. It is also written for parents who know or are about to discover that they overprotect in response to the neglect, abuse, or overprotection they themselves experienced in childhood.

In theory, most of us believe that in the twenty years or so that our children live with us, we would like to foster concrete skills and inner resources for independence. We know it is impossible and unwise to prevent our children from experiencing physical or emotional pain. In theory, we'll agree that if the goal is eventual independence, then overprotection is an inappropriate and ineffective parenting strategy for achieving it.

In theory.

In reality, we've seen how easily our theories about freedom and preparation for independence can go flying out the window.

> *Should I let Jamie go?*
> *Nothing bad has ever happened there.*
> *But if something happened to Jamie, I couldn't live with myself!*
> *So what am I supposed to do?*

(Jamie has not asked if she can join the Green Berets. She is four and wants to go to Lisa's bowling party in another part of town.)

For many of us, the easy, everyday parenting decisions have become too hard to make. Can the kids climb to the top of the jungle gym? Stay home alone? Travel by public transportation? Common sense tells us we ought to be wary of overprotection, but given the age we live in, given that we feel we can justify overprotection because "everybody else is doing it," it is becoming progressively more difficult to identify when protection turns to overprotection. Should we recognize we are being overprotective, we're tempted to defend ourselves saying "There's no alternative."

We think there's no alternative because we're no longer sure how to draw the thin line between sane caution and irrational overprotection. If just letting children go out the door can feel as if it requires an act of faith, is it any surprise that we're second-guessing our ability to make judgment calls?

Who knows what's safe? Who knows what's not? Uncertain, we're tempted to say "NO!" and keep the kids cocooned.

What exactly is overprotection, that approach to parenting from the no-no list that has become so commonplace? The way we think about overprotection has been evolving in the last fifty years. Webster's current definition reflects much of the earlier thinking: Overprotection is "undue or excessive protection or shielding, specifically an excessive restriction of a child's behavior allegedly in the interest of his health and welfare by an anxious, insecure or dominating mother."

The dictionary restricts overprotection to mothers, in particular to mothers who express their anxieties by dominating their children. For further confirmation, we are told to turn to the term *momism*, which links mothers and sons. Momism, we learn, refers to "an excessive popular adoration or oversentimentalization of mothers that is held to be oedipal in nature and is thought to allow overprotective or clinging mothers unconsciously to deny their offspring emotional emancipation and thus to set up psychoneurosis." The term *momism* was coined in 1942 by the American scientist and author Philip Wylie in his popular *Generation of Vipers*. It reflects the post–World War II anxiety that sons who had aggressive mothers replacing and overcompensating for the fathers who were away at war would turn out to be wimpy mama's boys, incapable of keeping their country safe for democracy when their own time came. Wylie claimed "mom" devours "her young in the firm belief that it is for their own good." She protects her son with her love, shielding him from normal childhood development and cushioning him from the challenges of becoming mature. "Mom" protects "her boy" not out of love for him, but out of love for herself.

In 1943 psychiatrist D. M. Levy published a popular study, *Maternal Overprotection*, based on an examination of more than two thousand case records with followup evaluations three, seven, and ten years later. In light of current views of the parent-child relationship, the increased participation of fathers as caregivers, and, in particular, the ways women are now defining what constitutes fulfillment in their lives, Dr. Levy's work seems out of date, with its references to aggressive maternal behavior, a woman's unresolved masculine drives, and penis envy. Nevertheless, certain of Dr. Levy's psychological explanations for what motivates and constitutes an overprotective attitude still appear to hold true, and while Dr. Levy does refer essentially to mothers as the primary caregivers, we might extend what he has to say about mothers to fathers as well.

Dr. Levy's overprotective parent monopolizes her child soon after birth. She "lives only for her child." Uncomfortable when she is away from the child for even the briefest time, she will allow no one else to train or handle the child, even her husband. With the baby as her excuse, she restricts her social life and sexual relationship with her spouse. Later, she may accompany her child to school, help him with his homework, and restrict him from most friendships, for they arouse her disapproval. For Levy, the following criteria characterize the overprotective relationship:

○ excessive contact (for instance, sleeping in the same bed with a child or frequently fondling him),
○ infantilization (delaying weaning beyond cultural expectations, waiting on a child hand and foot),
○ prevention of independent behavior (forbidding any vigorous play, restricting friendships, giving little responsibility), and either
○ insufficient maternal control (in which the parent is dominating and the child is anxiously obedient, submissive and overresponsive) or
○ excessive maternal control (in which the parent is indulgent and the child is impudent, demanding, and throws tantrums).

In a nutshell, Dr. Levy says the overprotective parent

holds her child tightly with one hand and makes the gesture of pushing away the rest of the world with the other. Her energies

> *are directed to preserving her infant as an infant for all times,*
> *preserving her baby from harm and from contact with the rest*
> *of humanity. For her child, she will fight hard, make every*
> *sacrifice. . . .*

Not coincidentally, most of the overprotective parents in Levy's study claimed that in their own youths they were deprived of "parental affection and of childhood play" and were burdened with responsibilities. Now, through their own children, they seek to recreate a "new childhood . . . free from all early privation," compensating for the love they were denied.

As recently as the late seventies, overprotection continued to be linked with maternal overinvestment. Writing in 1978, Nancy Chodorow, author of *The Reproduction of Mothering: Psychoanalysis and the Sociology of Gender*, explains that maternal overinvestment is perpetuated when women have exclusive responsibility for children. As far as female children are concerned, Chodorow wrote that "mother-daughter relationships in which the mother has no other adult support or meaningful work and remains ambivalently attached to her own mother produce . . . [an] inability to separate in daughters."

In search of a working definition of overprotection that includes men and women and reflects the way more parents are sharing the work of raising children, I find psychiatrist Theodore Isaac Rubin's definition most useful. For Dr. Rubin, overprotected children—boys or girls—are those who have been infantilized by their parents and consequently suffer deleterious effects. Rubin's overprotective parents are anxious, apprehensive, insecure, even paranoid. They may mistakenly believe it is preferable "to err on the side of overprotection rather than to be negligent." After all, they feel their overprotective behavior denotes love, while in fact, Rubin suggests, "many severely overprotecting parents actually feel intense repressed hostility toward their children because ordinary responsibility has been converted into a monstrous burden and the cause of unrelenting fear of impending catastrophe." Ultimately, Rubin understands that overprotection robs and exploits children: "It is a disease of the parent fostered on the child." The overprotected child is at risk for pathological consequences such as anxiety attacks and hypochondria long into adulthood. Self-esteem, in particular, is diminished, as overprotection "extends one's infancy and dependency way beyond the borders of necessity, resulting in atrophy of self on an intellectual, emotional and creative level."

Both Levy and Rubin describe overprotective parents and overprotected children they have encountered in therapeutic settings. Yet the majority of parents who overprotect now or are leaning toward overprotection won't necessarily come to a therapist's attention because the impact of overprotection doesn't always register until the child has grown up.

In order to understand contemporary overprotectors, we must look beyond the stereotypes—the monstrous or fretful mothers and the authoritative or controlling fathers. We need to stop labeling certain parents as being "naturally" overprotective or simply being "the overprotective type." Any one of us can exhibit overprotective attitudes and behaviors. We can be moved to overprotect by a particular child, by a particular issue that comes up, or by uncanny "vibes" we happen to be feeling. We overprotect to make peace with our past and present fears and our sense of inadequacy. And if we're not overprotecting at this moment, there's no assurance we won't ever begin.

We who currently overprotect—occasionally or around the clock—believe we do so differently than our parents and grandparents did. Mostly, we don't fret about our children having enough to eat. Medically sophisticated, we don't go into a tizzy over germs on doorknobs and toilet seats and the risk of getting chilled and "catching one's death of a cold." We're concerned about our children "making it" in the world, but that concern doesn't send us into a tailspin. Perhaps we've made it ourselves and feel equipped to guide them along the way; perhaps we've made it and have been disillusioned. Should we, along with our children, lose our cool when they apply to nursery school or college, we do know that not getting in to this school or that isn't the end of the world.

According to dozens of parents queried, it is safety in general and physical safety in particular that is the striking concern for most current overprotectors.

Observing myself as an overprotective parent and as an overprotected child, I have become more intensely convinced that *overprotection is neither benign nor innocuous, even when it is carried out in the name of love and justified by the exigencies of a threatening age.* Many of us have friends and relatives whom we think overprotect their children. We might complain to others, saying, "You would not believe how overprotective my brother is; he won't let his kids breathe!" Sometimes, we'll try to drop a hint: "Do you think a newborn baby really needs the heat turned up to seventy-five degrees?" or "Gee, when my children were that age, my husband and I left them with his parents for the weekend, and it really did turn out okay." Yet in most cases we usually hesitate to interfere with overprotective parents in any way at all, either because we assume that parents probably know what's best for their own children or because we rationalize that at least overprotection indicates the children are beloved and well cared for.

I think we need to reevaluate the way we stand by silently when we observe ourselves, our spouses, or other people we love overprotecting. Overprotection is not good for children in the short run or the long run, and that's simply the bottom line. If we restrict children from being touched by the world that might harm them, then we restrict them from the world that will touch their souls, delight them, intrigue them, open them to unconsidered possibilities.

Strategies to Restore Sane Protection

I knew I would have several tasks to accomplish before I could emerge from the state of hypervigilance that followed my car accident and stop overprotecting my own children. First I had to come to terms with the overprotection I had experienced as a child. I knew this would be a long process, one I had no choice but to pursue and think through. I found that writing diligently in a journal was my best resource, as it has successfully seen me through other phases of crisis, change, and growth.

Second, I found that I had to learn, as if from scratch, how parents protect their children and still let them go. Given how overprotection is so easily rationalized these days by our belief that the world is more dangerous than ever, that task was especially difficult. I needed to discover how to look rationally at any protective situation and decide the following:

○ Is this safe or not?
○ Is this important enough to my child to justify the risks entailed?
○ Is it possible to get my own fears and anxieties back under control?

I had a hunch, which proved correct, that I could learn how to protect and let go by listening hard to other people and getting a sense for what worked and what didn't. In the course of my investigations, I, with the help of my research assistant, Pamela Klassen, interviewed dozens of parents and children. Every encounter instructed me, but I was particularly enlightened by those parents who revealed how they made difficult protective decisions. By their example, I would discover how I might make peace with my own fears. Many children I interviewed revealed what made them feel safe and secure, and they reminded me how much children thrive with the right amount of independence.

The parents (or step-parents or other primary caregivers) who were interviewed fell into three groups. In the first group were those who admitted, some proudly and some sheepishly, to being the "overprotective type." A second group said that they were given to overprotection only in particular areas or that they overprotected a particular child who was especially vulnerable because of personality or physical health. In the third group, some said they were genuinely not burdened by fears for their children. Others in this final group said they were indeed fearful but consciously kept their fears "in check" or "censored" so their children could "taste life."

The children (middle-school, senior-high, college-age, and adult children) were raised by parents in all three groups. I asked all the children to reflect on how their own parents protected them and gave them a feeling of being safe. I asked adults how *their* parents' fears might connect to the fears they felt today as adults. If they were overprotected, I asked them to explore how that continues to have an impact on their lives.

The questions adults were asked inevitably touched raw nerves. Frequently they didn't realize how much they had to say until they got going: "The topic of overprotection opens up a can of worms" was a typical response. In my interviews, I proceeded with caution, particularly when startling connections made between the past and the present aroused unresolved anger or overwhelming sadness.

Based on these interviews and responses to questionnaires (for the most part I have either obscured identities or created composites based on similar profiles), as well as on interviews with experts in child psychology, family counseling, and anthropology of religion, I learned how

O to think through protective issues with more objectivity, which was different from my previous method of child rearing: the approach of reacting to what my own parents had done to me by doing the opposite to my children;

○ to distinguish my real from my irrational fears;

○ to trust how well my husband and I generally complemented each other as protectors; and

○ to reassure myself, to think through my panic and transform it into appropriate vigilance.

I believe that the parents and children I consulted spoke with me as openly and generously as they did because they trusted their stories might make a difference to others. Honoring their trust, I share these lives and the stories I was told in the hope that you may come to understand, as I did, that when protection turns to overprotection, regardless of how we rationalize, regardless of how and why it was motivated, regardless of how much our culture might equate the overprotective parent with the "good, loving parent," it has serious, long-term consequences for a child's self-esteem and sense of well-being.

I believe that if we are out-of-control overprotectors or once-in-a-while overprotectors, it is possible to understand and confront our fears, consider and redesign our behavior, and still keep our children safe by teaching ourselves to let go at the right times and in the right places.

In part 1, we'll be exploring how parents can easily rationalize overprotection. Next, we'll begin to recognize what overprotective parenting looks like and consider some of the sad effects overprotection has upon children—and even grandchildren.

In part 2, I offer a guide for evaluating and persevering through some of the most frequent protective challenges parents face at each stage of a child's development. Here you'll also encounter parents of children with special needs, who have succeeded in protecting their children and respecting their right to have freedom. (Please note that throughout this book, while

I often refer to a child's parents as "father" and "mother," I do recognize the changing configuration of families: We can no longer assume that the persons primarily responsible for a child are either married to each other or are of different sexes.)

In the course of fashioning myself into a capable and thoughtful protector, I have turned to the wisdom and strategies that parents from diverse religious and cultural backgrounds have evolved over the ages to unburden themselves of overwhelming fears. Obviously, parents at the close of the twentieth century are not the first ever to channel their fears. In part 3, I investigate the powerful customs, prayers, and ceremonies parents have relied upon. These rituals acknowledge the fears parents have for their children and give them language and form to provide blessings for their children to guard them as they go forth into the world. We can use, adapt, or redesign these rituals for our own purposes. As a matter of fact, many of us are already performing some of these rituals without being aware of it.

I hope you will read about concerns that other parents have that mirror your own and hear fears with which you are intimate. I trust that you can adapt some of these strategies and ceremonies to your own life and that they will make a difference to you and your children as you draw that very thin line between protection and overprotection.

2

How We Rationalize
Overprotection

Many of us now raising children believe the world isn't as safe as it used to be. It's crazier, we say, more violent than ever.

Yet if we compare ouselves to our own parents (the folks we called "uptight"), we may discover we're more anxious, restrictive, and intrusive than they ever were. As one suburban mother who waits for the school bus each morning with her thirteen-year-old son says, "I must stand between my child and a coarse, uncaring world."

Why do so many parents now believe that children are at greater risk? What are we referring to when we describe the world as being more dangerous? How does our perception of danger determine the way we protect our children?

We might wistfully recall a childhood in which crimes didn't happen in broad daylight in the neighborhoods where nice people lived. With our parents' blessings, we were always venturing outdoors, prowling through empty lots, just goofing off. When we got hurt, we went back home and found a parent; otherwise some neighbor, even one we hardly knew, provided the bandage.

In that childhood of memory, a parent could grant a child autonomy because the consensus was that the home, the neighborhood, and the world of one's town were safe and hospitable to children. Helen, who grew up during World War II in a small town, was given a pony and cart and in the winter a sleigh. From the age of eight, she would take all-day excursions within a five-mile radius of the town, limited only by her concern for her pony's stamina.

We may remember being in charge of our own fun. Robert, growing up in the fifties, recalls being outdoors all day. "I liked to be by myself, just doing what I wanted." After dinner, Robert would run outside to play stickball on the street with the kids, and his parents would say, "Be home at eight o'clock." They never asked "Where are you going?" or "Who are you playing with?" His time was unaccounted for. When a parent called to a child playing in the woods and the child didn't answer, it was because the child was out of earshot.

Even coddled, urban children may recall having had full, independent lives. Celia, a teenager in the sixties, says her parents, whom she ranks in the "ninety-ninth percentile of over-protectors," still allowed her to go by subway with a girlfriend from Brooklyn to Manhattan to see all the Broadway plays. At night, they'd return by subway and walk the two blocks home. "Today," says Celia, "no one would dream of letting a high-school girl do what I did."

Many parents assumed perfect strangers would come to the aid of their children. At nine years of age, Ruth would travel alone by train to her grandmother's house, holding her valise and violin. A mere slip of a girl, her baggage overwhelmed her. Her parents had told her that if she conducted herself like a little lady, some kind gentleman would come to her aid. And one always did. "He'd take my suitcase and carry it for me," says Ruth. "I didn't worry he would steal my violin. Or steal me."

It's no surprise, then, that in such a climate Margaret Mead could write a government pamphlet in 1962 advising parents that "children will do things on their own if adults establish safe pathways for them, which end in a park or a wood, a museum, a fair, a hill to climb, a cave to explore." Parents were told to let their adolescent children learn to move farther away from home by "packing their own rucksacks . . . learning how to be resourceful, how to avoid emergencies and how to meet them when they occur." Mead encouraged parents to tell their children that they must be free to follow all paths, no matter where they lead.

A wood? A cave? we ask today, feeling the long distance we have traveled. *Are you kidding? Over my dead body!*

Do these anecdotes of carefree childhoods really confirm that parents of a generation or two back were strangers to worry? While it's true that many parents could once give children more physical autonomy, parents before us had their own giant concerns, which gnawed at some and overwhelmed or consumed others. Jackie Leo, editor in chief of *Family Circle*, writes, "When I was growing up, parents and children harbored two particular fears. The first was unthinkable—the possibility of an all-out nuclear war. The other was also tragic, but more personal—the epidemic of polio." We can't forget that parents who came before us had the very same core worries that keep us awake:

> Will my child be healthy and live a long life?
> Will my child travel safely from place to place?
> Will my child manage without me, learning what's necessary to survive, eat, and find shelter?
> Will my child marry and have love and companionship and give birth to children in my lifetime?
> Will my child have friends and not enemies?
> Will my child be happy and lucky?
> Will my child have the inner resources to emerge from setbacks?
> Will my child live in peaceful times?
> Will my child become an ethical, law-abiding, honorable person who will make me proud and not ashamed?

Will my child carry on my values?
Will my child remain connected to our family and
maintain and respect our culture?

We might put our current sense of danger in perspective if
we consider American childhood in the early 1800s. In colonial
days, before the medical specialty called pediatrics had been
created, infants died frequently of digestive ailments referred
to as the bloody flux, the watery gripes, the summer sickness,
and cholera infantum. They died of tuberculosis, and in the
South they died of the "burning ague," malaria. If children
didn't die of sickness, they may have died of dangerous or
ineffective cures—of home remedies combining over-the-
counter mercury and opium, of the ever-popular leechings, of
powdered chalk in gruel to cure diarrhea, of pewter filings in
treacle to remove worms, of a hot roasted onion applied to
the ear for earache.

Colonial children lucky enough to escape disease might still
be burned by their kitchen fireplaces or by fires set off by
candles. If infants slept with their parents or nurses, as many
did, they could be smothered. It was not uncommon for children to fall down the family's well or be trampled by horses'
hooves.

If we shift into the present time, one might think we'd feel
more at ease, for in addition to the medical knowledge we
freely turn to, we have a panoply of protective products for
baby-proofing our living spaces and better shielding our children from common daily disasters. The Safety 1st company
alone, which offered the popular Baby on Board signs for cars,
now advertises a line of products for child safety, which includes garbage disposal–switch locks, furniture-corner cush-
ions, fireplace-edge bumpers, small-object testers, toilet locks,
bathtub-knob covers, floating bathtub thermometers, smoke
and fire alarms, cases for dangling shoelaces, and pads to cushion babies' knees. In some cities, Americans are hiring profes-

sional child-proofers who will evaluate a home for safety and provide and install the appropriate child-proofing paraphernalia. Some parents oblige their children to carry cellular phones or hitch them to transmitters that monitor their whereabouts.

One would think our medicine, technology, and gadgetry might put us at ease; but almost nothing seems to increase our confidence, persuade us to rein in our anxiety, or enable us to make letting go of our children a priority, or even a goal.

Danger, from a parent's perspective, is about perception. The anxiety provoked by a realistic and potential danger affects us in the same way as the anxiety provoked by an imagined danger. If we *perceive* that the world we are bringing our children into and preparing them to face is scarier than ever before, then we conclude that the protective measures we take are always going to fall short.

One might think that common sense would tell us that our acute awareness of danger is out of sync with the likelihood that the danger will, in fact, come to pass. We have drunken drivers, but we have seatbelts. We have threatening diseases, but we have powerful antibiotics, radiation treatments, and chemotherapies. We have new psychological pressures, complicated demands on our lives, and in general less support from our extended families; but even as lay people, we have become astute psychologically and sociologically, and we have literature, support groups, and clinics to turn to for professional assistance. Politically speaking, the world remains volatile, but as I write, young Americans are not about to go off to war.

Still, we remain convinced that our protective measures will always be insufficient because our children can encounter unexpected, unanticipatable danger anywhere: in their bedrooms, their kitchens, their classrooms, their backyards, their bus stops, their playgrounds—let alone one mile or a thousand miles away from home. I believe it is the loss of these settings as safety zones that has sent us over the edge and distinguished us from the generations of parents before us.

When twelve-year-old Polly Klass of Petaluma, California, was abducted in October of 1993, she had been playing a board game with school friends in her bedroom. Her mother was at home, asleep down the hall. When Polly's body was found two months later, reporter Jane Gross wrote that this kidnapping had touched so many people "because of its night-mare quality—for parents who assume that the one place their children are safe is at home, and for children who dread the evil stranger in their bedroom." We don't pay attention to the statistics that might assure us that very few children are actually abducted each year. If abduction happens at all, we are con-vinced it will happen to our child.

Be sure, we parents who hold that we live in especially fearful times are not worry addicts who have nothing better to do than compulsively fabricate catastrophes and worst-case scenarios: We recall Tylenol laced with cyanide; we thought we were sup-posed to shake cans of Pepsi to listen for hypodermic needles; we witnessed tiny school children huddled in a dark elevator the day the Twin Towers were bombed, and we saw the real thing over and over on newscasts and again in the made-for-TV movie, further engraving the image in our memories.

It's common to blame the media for having exacerbated our fears and created a sense that danger is all around us. Surely we all know what it means to have our eyes and ears barraged with terrifying information of crimes committed against children—crimes that are bloodier, grizzlier, and more brazen than before. Susan, mother of a three-year-old, says that when she's been inattentive to media coverage, she goes about her day, her awareness of dangers to children suppressed. But once she hears or reads about a horrible event and is confronted with it repeatedly, she becomes so fearful that harm will come to her child that she feels reluctant to take him anywhere.

Some news items will shake us up more than others, and

we find ourselves vicariously experiencing the horror and vulner-ability of the victim and the devastating sorrow of the victim's parents. I recall being especially shaken after learning about fif-teen-year-old Zipora Yagpdajev, who went out on a morning walk in the Williamsburg neighborhood of Brooklyn in Decem-ber of 1990. Raymond Vargas, who tried to rob her for money to buy heroin, strangled Zipora when she tried to run away. He set her body on fire on a steel catwalk suspended from the deck of the Williamsburg Bridge. I found myself equally unnerved to hear that in March of 1992, seventeen-year-old Francisco Ortiz of the Bronx was stabbed to death in a brawl, apparently a racial attack, on a city bus. The suspected killer was a sixteen-year-old boy who lived three blocks away from Francisco. According to Francisco's older brother, "When my father heard, he just wanted to throw himself off a bridge."

But not every parent blames the media for the extent of our terror. Ed, a physician's assistant and father of a son, is con-vinced that lawlessness and violence have actually increased. Ed asks, "Did you read about that twenty-one-year-old woman who just graduated from Princeton with honors, a lieutenant in the army, this golden girl, who was shot to death by a fellow soldier? She refused to dance with him and he killed her. The next thing, you see a picture in the newspaper of her father kneeling at her coffin in Arlington Cemetery. It's even worse among young kids. Did you read about the ten-year-old boy in Detroit who robbed and killed a pregnant mother? The seven-year-old boys who raped a six-year-old girl at school? We're dealing with a society with no rules, where kids grow up without consciences: They'll hurt, maim, rob, rape, whatever they want with no thought or remorse. If you happen to be in the wrong spot or look at someone wrong, you're in trouble."

Federal Bureau of Investigation statistics partially support Ed's perceptions. Though violent crime, in general, has leveled off since 1990, there has been a 47 percent increase from 1988 to 1992 in arrests of people under eighteen years of age for violent crimes. In 1992 alone, 3400 people in America were killed by young people.

We are particularly horrified when we hear about violence committed by young people in schools, because we had long considered school to be a sanctuary—a reliable, safe public space, the extension of our own home. If school violence was once limited to the urban landscape, to graffiti-scarred schools surrounded by burned-out buildings and vacant lots, it has escalated and spread everywhere. Each week, we see the headlines, "Innocent School Children Shot . . ." It is very possible that the kid who sits next to your child in algebra is carrying a pocket knife, a box opener, or a .22-caliber semiautomatic with nineteen rounds of ammunition. It is very possible that your child's classmates who once "resolved" their conflicts through fistfights and even knives are now "resolving" them with handguns. According to a 1989 Justice Department survey of more than ten thousand students, school violence appears to have become as prevalent in the suburbs and rural areas as it is in the cities. While 8 percent of urban students interviewed said they were victims of violent crimes in school, 7 percent of suburban and rural students said that they also were. The responses were just as close for students who said they were victims of theft at school, for students who feared attacks at or en route to school, for students who feared going to certain places in their schools, and for students who took a weapon or other object with them to class for protection.

Neither the school ensconced in a hamlet nor the school tucked into a suburb is exempt from violence. In the recent past, a high-school freshman in suburban Dartmouth, Massachusetts, was stabbed to death by three schoolmates armed with a baseball bat, a billy club, and a hunting knife. In Walton, New York, a ninth-grade English teacher was shot in the face by a fifteen-year-old boy who had been told to stop talking or leave the room. Two seventh graders in Lorain, Ohio, had plotted to stab their English teacher with a butcher knife. Eight nine- to thirteen-year-olds in a Yonkers, New York, elementary school were charged with sexually assaulting a twelve-year-old girl while "playing a rape game" on the school playground.

School systems are responding to violence by installing metal detectors, forming school district police forces, using dogs trained to detect drugs and guns, setting up hot lines to encourage students to report those who carry weapons, creating parent patrols to create safe pathways to and from school, and instituting programs teaching nonviolent forms of conflict resolution. Just knowing these extreme measures are necessary heightens our anxiety. And if the experts are right—that the increase in school violence can be linked to poverty, abuse, and neglect; to kids raised in single-parent homes; and to the profusion of violence in movies and television—then no end to the profusion of this kind of violence, and no end to our anxiety, seems to be in sight.

Drugs, Alcohol, Sex

For parents of preteens and teenagers, the availability of drugs and alcohol and the life-threatening prospect of unprotected sex further heighten the perception that the world is unmanageably dangerous. With substance abuse, we contend with damage that is potentially permanent. And we all know, having once been teenagers ourselves, that the warnings of parents are easily sloughed off because they seem so old-fashioned, so hysterical, so out of touch with reality. "Drugs and alcohol are all around them," says George, a stepfather of two teenage daughters. George doesn't trust his daughters will heed his warnings: He knows they're not immune to friends who'll convince them to experiment or immune to their own curiosity. "Just because they're my children, and I believe they're good kids, I can't ever think they won't take drugs or drink." In the back of his mind, George wonders, "What if they fall in with the wrong crowd? Would they keep a secret from us: Could something upset them so much that they'd turn to drugs?"

George's level of concern about substance abuse for his daughters comes nowhere close to his concern about their sexual activity, and many parents of teens would concur. George sucks in his breath: "I can't talk about it." If he had his "druthers," he'd discourage dating until college. George knows, and so does every parent, that a teenager might get off drugs, recover from substance abuse, enter rehabilitation, get another chance to start life over; but sex is about AIDS, and AIDS is about death.

Beverly, a mother of two, recalls that before she went to college in 1970, her father asked their family doctor to put her on the pill. "My father's biggest fear was that I would get pregnant and it would ruin my life." In retrospect, this concern seems daintily Victorian to Beverly. "Remember how people used to whisper the words 'she got into trouble' or 'home for unwed mothers'? They'd terrify us with images of illegal abortions done in seedy backrooms with coat hangers. But after *Row v. Wade* in 1973, if a twenty-year-old girl gets pregnant, no one is happy, but it's not the end of her life. I worry that if my son and daughter have unprotected sex, they will get AIDS. With AIDS, there are no second chances."

Beverly's son is only twelve and her daughter is fourteen, so you'd think her worry is premature. It's not. According to health experts, more than 33 percent of fifteen-year-old boys and 27 percent of fifteen-year-old girls have had intercourse. Among sexually active girls, 61 percent have had multiple partners. Teenagers may think they're immortal, but the facts say otherwise: Twenty percent of all AIDS patients are under twenty years old. Beverly has already had both her children inoculated against hepatitis B, which can be transmitted through sexual contact. "My children are pretty naive right now, and they know exactly how I feel about waiting to have sex until they're married, but I have to be realistic. Kids in their school are pressured to have sex by the time they graduate high school. My kids aren't going to give me a few days' warning before they succumb to peer pressure so I can get them a doctor's appointment."

In 1983, when Beverly's children were small, she hired a sixteen-year-old baby-sitter to accompany the family to the shore. She asked the sitter's mother if there were any restrictions she should put on the sitter when she had time off. The mother, a laid-back woman, said her daughter could walk along the beach with her boyfriend and stay out as late as she wished. Only one thing was forbidden: She couldn't drive with this boy because he drank. "I must have had my mouth wide open," says Beverly, "because the mother went on to explain, 'The consequences of sex are reversible. The consequences of being killed in a crash with a drunken driver are not.'" Beverly muses, "What would that mother say now?"

Toxicity All Around

We throw up our hands each time we get more bad news about the toxic potential of many of the natural and synthetic substances we surround ourselves with and rely upon. A rude turnabout has been played on those of us who followed the tried and true ways of our parents and grandparents. Forget the homey, natural, commonsense things we once thought were good and safe for children in unlimited amounts—sunshine! a healthy tan! a nice glass of cold whole milk! fresh fruits and vegetables! fresh water from the tap! They turn out to be potential health hazards to humans, and particularly to children, who are so much more vulnerable. Expose children to the sun's ultraviolet rays without adequate sunscreen and you increase their chances of getting skin cancer. Some parents worry that recombinant bovine somatotropin, an artificial growth hormone given to cows to stimulate milk production, may have been approved for use before adequate testing on humans has been completed. We hear that fresh fruits and vegetables doused with pesticides to improve agricultural production carry poisons. Tap water, if it's contaminated by lead that has leeched from older pipes, has been shown to damage a child's nervous system, depressing his or her intelligence and ability to learn.

Whether or not we act on this information and take precautionary measures, we live with the possibility that we are raising our children in toxic environments and feeding them poisoned foods. Each week, as we turn to the science pages of the newspaper, we discover it's time to plaster a skull and crossbones over yet another formerly trustworthy commodity. Debra Lynn Dadd, author of *The Nontoxic Home and Office*, reports that phenol, an ingredient in furniture and floor polish, is suspected of causing cancer in humans. Formaldehyde, present in no-iron bed linens, permanent press clothing, and particleboard furniture, is suspected of causing cancer and birth defects. According to Dadd, humans can develop cancer if they are exposed to the nitrates in foods, food treated with pesticides, barbecued and broiled foods, microwaves, electromagnetic fields caused by the electric wires and appliances in our homes (not just the microwave ovens we "nuke" with but the old staples: the television sets, electric blankets, electric clocks). Treat children to fast-food hamburgers, and if they're made of tainted meat, as they were at the Jack in the Box restaurant in Seattle, they could die. What's in the toothpaste we're obliging our child to use three times a day? What's in the finish on the wooden swing set we've installed out back? What will experts turn up tomorrow? Margarine is *not* better than butter—it's worse? Will they change their minds again? How can we ever rest assured about anything?

We joke that experts will soon be telling us a diet rich in fruits and vegetables and low in saturated fats is deadly. When the old advice is wrong and the new advice gets reversed or revised each week, we don't know whom to trust: the American Academy of Pediatrics? our family doctor? journalists on the health beat? Our loss of trust and confidence in experts only compounds our case of the jitters. If experts can't decide conclusively what's good for our children, how are we, who can't run a biochemical analysis, supposed to decide? If experts tell us that the electromagnetic fields from high-voltage power lines above our children's school are among the strongest in the state but then add that they're uncertain if exposure to electromagnetic fields poses a cancer threat—or any threat at all—what are we supposed to do? Move out of the community? Move the school? Spend millions of dollars to bury the power lines? Try to forget about the whole thing?

No One to Trust

To complicate already complicated matters, we believe we do the work of protecting alone, unlike our parents, who trusted in the kindness of strangers, the compassion of neighbors, and in the virtue of teachers, clergy, family doctors, and dentists. We doubt anyone outside our immediate family will look out for our children as we do. This makes us especially edgy if we must depend on day-care centers and baby-sitters. Perhaps the first time we heard about molestations in daycare centers, allegations about violent nannies and abuse by satanic cults, reports of sexual misconduct among parish priests, we said to ourselves, "Well, that's a fluky thing that happens to other people in other places." Certainly, we believed, at least we can trust *our* own baby-sitters, *our* nursery school teachers, and we had enough reverence for *our* own clergy to assume they were beyond reproach.

Then something snapped. We heard one story too many about perverted people who, on the outside, couldn't have seemed more loving, more ethical, more harmless. Now we may assume all people have malevolent intentions toward our children until proven otherwise. If our children tell us stories about a teacher's erratic behavior or use of sexually suggestive language, we do not chalk it up to a child's overactive imagination: we investigate. With regret, we instruct our principals to caution teachers, even the kindergarten teachers, "No touching, no hugging, no hair tousling."

Abduction

Abduction, regardless of any actual statistics, regardless of the likelihood that it could actually happen, is the prime source of anxiety for parents of younger children. "My daughters are so vulnerable," says Jorge, a father who worries his two daughters will be cajoled into a car and never be seen again. Kate worries her four-year-old son Jeff will be abducted at the mall because he's so adorable. She's started shopping for food on weekends when her husband can stay home with Jeff, and shops for her own clothes through catalogs.

Abduction, according to journalist Noelle Oxenhandler, is "the ultimate horror for parents, for it accomplishes in a single hour a realization that under normal circumstances is the work of years and years: the realization that our children have a fate that is separate from our own. This realization is difficult enough when that fate is a pleasant one." Oxenhandler tells us that the horror goes even deeper than the "absolute rupture": "It is a primal horror, in that it actualizes the ancient fear of being carried off by an evil stranger."

The closer to home the incidents hit, the more fervently we believe that it could strike there again. Last month my neighbor Carla heard that a ten-year-old boy who lived near our park was nearly abducted. A rusty old truck had stopped soon after the boy got out of his schoolbus. The driver beckoned to him then tried to pull him inside. Fortunately, the boy screamed and got away and ran home to his mother. "This is not supposed to happen here," says Carla, "but it just did!"

Danger Everywhere

In our current state of mind, we take no aspect of our child's everyday safety for granted. Danger, we believe, lurks in every bite, every breath, every relationship, every move our kids make. We don't assume any school, any caretaker, any teacher is safe.

We can't hear about a tragedy befalling a child anywhere and convince ourselves, "That was a freak occurrence; it won't happen to my child." Every incident startles us into a nightmare mode, and we imagine the tragedy will happen to our children. There is no place to get away from it all, no pure hilltop. Lacking safe havens, lacking any time or place to let down our guard, we hold our hearts in our mouths as we attempt to protect our children. Since we feel we can't anticipate where and when danger will erupt, we can't dodge it or cordon it off in time. Feeling powerless and out of control, we overprotect.

Ideally, we'd get our act together and accustom ourselves to the kind of risks our children now face and provide them with the appropriate skills to avoid or confront danger. Instead, many of us are in too startled a state of mind to teach survival and independence. We may claim that overprotection is the only response we are capable of, and, to be honest, when the situation is so awful and so poignant, such an assessment is frankly persuasive.

It is sad, writer Elizabeth Crow comments, "that as society has become more complicated and violent, and as the problems confronting us seem more resistant to social change, we gravitate toward short-term solutions that may combat anxiety, but do little to remedy the root causes of our distress."

Overprotection is one such short-term solution. Overwhelmed with fears for our children, we maintain that if protection is a good thing, overprotection is even better. This isn't necessarily so, and we know it. In fact, according to Karla Hull, author of *Safe Passage: A Guide for Teaching Children Personal Safety*, "it is this very act of overprotectiveness that may be making our children more vulnerable. The overprotective parent conveys the idea that the world is full of dangers that the child cannot handle. Thus the underlying message of overprotection is that a child is not competent. This significantly undermines the child's self-esteem, increasing his feeling of helplessness in dangerous situations."

There's yet another reason we gravitate toward overprotection. In numerous cultures, the overprotective parent is held up as the model of goodness, caring, and devotion. While overprotective parents may be chided for excessive doting, exaggerated selflessness or out-of-control anxiety, they are rarely villified. In most cultures, the overprotector is placed in the elevated subset of all good, loving parents deserving of approbation. As a matter of fact, the overprotective parent often represents the selfless parent par excellence and is held up for emulation. In Egypt, for instance, according to Sari, raised in Cairo, "Egyptians praise the overprotective mother for sacrificing her own life and happiness for her children. By overprotecting, she shows how much she cares. If she didn't make a fuss over her children eating well and eating on time and fuss over their coming in from play at a good hour, people might criticize her, saying, 'She is a selfish woman who only cares about having her own fun.'"

A recent multipage magazine advertisement for a Nissan minivan shows how Americans rationalize overprotection. On the first page, a little girl walks into a shallow, rippling body of water wearing a plastic blow-up tube around her waist. The text reads, "You hold your child's hand when she crosses the street, you won't let her climb to the top of the jungle gym and you make her wear a life preserver in the kiddie pool." Flip to the two-page spread that follows and you see a bold headline, "Have we got a minivan for you," and underneath it the words, "Think of us as very over-protective parents." I imagine the advertisers intend to suggest that if you are the kind of committed parent who truly cares about your child, are there for her in places where you're not necessary and ready to curtail any activity that hints of danger, then you will surely take the safety of a family car with appropriate seriousness.

The ad affirms the parent who hovers underneath a jungle gym, teaching a child that climbing high is just too risky and, hence, lowering all her horizons. And a life preserver in a wading pool? Pity the poor child so humiliated in front of her friends, corseted in unnecessary protection, separated out by intrusive parents for ineptitude.

This advertisement depicts overprotection as an endearing expression of love and concern. True enough: Overprotection can be motivated by a parent's devotion and selflessness, a parent's willingness to act as a shield and barrier against all harm. Nonetheless, a loving and concerned parent fosters a child's sense of competence, independence, and trust in the world, critical skills for survival and happiness. Overprotection ignores or undermines these skills.

Finally, in wording the headline "Have we got a van for you," in Yenta the Matchmaker's Yiddish-like intonation, the ad implies that the most intense overprotection is practiced by Jewish mothers, and this might lead us to think that overprotection has a single face. Let's set the record straight from the start: Jewish mothers—mine included—are indeed well known for acts of outlandish overprotection, particularly against physical danger. Stereotypical images of a Jewish mother's protectiveness have been popularized by borscht-belt comedians and by literary characters such as Mrs. Portnoy and Mrs. Morningstar. Nonetheless, Jewish mothers have not cornered the market on overprotection in America. I have seen Jewish mothers matched and outshined in every category of overprotective furor and industry by Jewish fathers (it is my Jewish brother-in-law, who once dressed his baby son in two woolen hats and a hood on a winter day, who comes readily to mind. My sister lamented, "I've married my mother.") In the course of my interviews, I've seen overprotective Jewish fathers and mothers equaled in the intensity of their unbridled worries and broad restrictions by parents of every nationality, race, and religion. Obviously, each culture has its own specific language of overprotective gestures for articulating the most compelling fears accrued in its history: including the fear of hunger, poverty, of totalitarian regimes, of bias-crimes, of discrimination, of assimilation.

Curiously enough, even if we're aware of the negative consequences of overprotection, we trust those consequences can be reversed. As one mother told me, "It's too bad I overprotect my daughter because she's missing out on fun and good experiences. When she's thirty, she can go into therapy and get over it. I'd rather know that I've kept her alive until then." Thirty years of overprotection don't peel off children as easily as undershirts. Problems linked to overprotection, such as depression, social anxiety, agoraphobia, obesity, and panic disorders, are not readily resolved. Moreover, it goes on and on: Children who are stifled and denied autonomy are likely to grow into parents who intrude upon their children's lives.

We desperately need perspective on protection. My neighbor, a grandmother in her seventies, when passing me in the public library, said, "When my children were young, so this was over forty years ago, I went to a lecture with a psychologist in this very building, and he told us that when mothers felt ambivalence toward their children, they overprotected them to compensate. He said that's how mothers made up for any love they didn't feel or distracted themselves from facing the truth: that being a parent wasn't the end-all satisfaction. That's what we thought then. But now," this grandmother says, tapping at my collar with a sharp index finger, "the young parents are saying that with the world as dangerous as it is, can we call any form of protection overprotection?" Softly, she says to me, "Honey, even then, there must be a limit. How can I tell my son and daughter they're going overboard protecting their children?"

Listen to what she's saying: We've become so obsessed by keeping our children safe and alive that we've lost sight of other equally compelling responsibilities we have toward them. Our extreme terror cannot justify overprotection. To protect is a response and a responsibility. To overprotect is a response gone awry.

3

Overprotective Parents, Overprotected Children

The Parents

There is no single way parents overprotect. Overprotection can be extreme, intense, and consistent. It can be subtle or sporadic, conscious or unconscious, proud or defensive, present in the face of certain issues and absent in others. Despite the variety, we readily spot the overprotector in action. We'll note the salient lack of correspondence between the parent's fears and the real dangers a child might realistically face. We'll note unnecessary intrusiveness.

Meet Frederick, considered by his friends to be the most overprotective parent of their crowd. It's the way he hovers and fusses in a fenced-in suburban back yard that leads me to pick him out among the other parents at a barbecue; it's the way he treats his seven-year-old Brian and toddler Amanda as though they had just been rescued from drowning or liberated from a dismal orphanage. They are healthy, clever children, I have been told, born without problems or medical fanfare (no previous miscarriages, no prematurity, no infertility treatments, no test-tube technology). For Frederick, this is not a brief spell of overprotectiveness that comes and goes after a crisis, a calamity, a medical episode, or a specific worry—it is overprotection as a constant stance.

When I later visit Frederick, a thirty-six-year-old investment consultant who works from his home, he turns off his computer and bolts from his desk as Brian and Amanda amble in. He clutches them to his chest, startled by their vitality and by his own overwhelming passion for them. Tickling their tummies with his bushy salt-and-pepper hair and beard, he whispers endearments: "Angel, Pumpkin!" If there's a school trip, I learn, Frederick takes off from work and drives Brian to the planetarium or petting farm, following behind the school bus his son must not board, for, as he says, "Who knows the whole truth of a bus driver's driving record?" To assure me he isn't paranoid, Frederick keys his worry to facts. In frighteningly vivid detail, he tells me about a chartered bus, carrying seventh- and eighth-graders returning home to Long Island from a school trip to Montreal, that slid off a slushy highway in the Adirondacks, tumbled down an embankment, plunged into a ravine, and killed two children. The driver, going at least ten miles over the speed limit on slick roads, had a record of accidents and moving violations. "In a sane world, this man would have his license revoked. In our world," says Frederick, "he drives children."

I join Frederick, Brian, and his friend for a walk on a quiet country road. Frederick entrusts Amanda to his wife, Shelly, only after reminding her to put sunscreen on Amanda and keep her hydrated with bottled—not tap—water. Shelly rolls her eyes; apparently it is easier to go along with Frederick's overprotective policies than to negotiate.

Having lost ourselves in gossip about a mutual friend, Frederick catches himself and notices that Brian and his friend have managed to get far ahead of us. I'm reminded of how I once gradually learned to go places by myself: by first walking to the park a few steps ahead of my young uncles, Effie and Shep, who—bless them—knowing how overprotective my parents were, took it upon themselves to treat me to freedom and instruct me in the most rudimentary survival skills whenever they were put in charge of me. I felt very brave and grown-up as I remembered to turn at the correct corner and to stick my head out demonstrably to the right and left before crossing. When I arrived at my grandparents' house, shocked by my own success, I ran around broadcasting, "I came here all by myself," as if I were Admiral Perry at the North Pole. As a parent, I would eventually trail behind my own daughters once they had learned enough about cars, roads, and strangers, in an effort to prepare them to wend their own ways home from friends' houses.

Frederick shouts piercingly to Brian: "Freeze! You must always be in my line of vision."

We are less than a block away from the boys and there isn't a car in sight. The children stand frozen like statues. Identifying deeply with Brian I blurt out, "Let him breathe!"

"I'd be a fool to take chances," Frederick tells me, taking large strides to reach the boys. "Life is too fragile." For Frederick, intensified parental concern doesn't just come at limited junctures such as when the children first go to kindergarten, are going off to college, or recovering from a concussion. For Frederick, each moment of each day feels like a critical juncture, and the urge to control by overprotecting is irresistible.

I imagine Brian must feel humiliated to be treated in this way in front of his friend. My heart goes out to Brian when I consider his future: What will happen when he grows up and it's time to move far beyond his father's line of vision? What confidence, what optimism, what self-assurance, what survival skills will he have then? What if Brian knows only how vulnerable he is to real and imagined fears? How will Brian separate himself from his father's fears and let them go? Frederick is not teaching Brian how to distinguish between those situations that are truly dangerous and those that pose a negligible risk. When parents see risk everywhere and constantly take precautions to avert danger, they train their children to feel constantly endangered.

Frederick, however, has no doubts that he is acting in his children's best interest. For Frederick, there is no such thing as protection that's out of proportion; there is no fine line to cross over.

Of course Frederick is reacting to real and imagined dangers, but I can't help but wonder: Could his overprotectiveness also reflect his reaction to an abscess of pain or emptiness that lies under the surface? Many parents who overprotect are compensating, through their children, for some critical ingredient missing in their childhoods, whether it be love, attention, warmth, kindness, sense of safety, or maybe good fortune. Attentive beyond measure to their own children, the compensating parents will shield them bodily from the abuses, absences, or sadnesses they once knew—regardless of the fact that their children are not experiencing the same challenges they faced, nor are they likely to. They will use their children as stand-ins for themselves, raising them with overprotection to undo or rectify their own pain. Does this hyperattentiveness and shielding provide healing for parents, giving them a feeling that they are repairing the world? Maybe it does. The noxious side effect is that what may be therapeutic for parents can be disabling to children.

What kinds of life stories might undergird an overprotective stance? Colleen, a parent whose life revolves around overprotecting her child, Shawn, willingly articulates the connection between her own past and her child: "I'm trying to give him all the love and attention I didn't get." One of five children, Colleen lost her father when she was twelve. As Colleen recalls, without her father, the warmth and cohesiveness in the family were gone. Her mother, a cold person, grew even more remote. As she worked around the clock in a restaurant, the children fended for themselves.

"You can split your love many ways," says Colleen, "but you can't split your time and attention and be involved with five children. The sun didn't rise and set on any of us. My mother never knew the foods or teachers I loved or hated. It sounds petty, but it was huge for me."

Today, Colleen appears to have no other strong interests outside of Shawn. If she goes out once every six months without him, that's a lot. She hardly trusts her husband with Shawn and agonizes when she sends Shawn to a nursery during the two days she works. Colleen maintains she's just trying to show Shawn how much she loves him so he can have the love he needs—love she feels she never had.

If Colleen overprotects to compensate for missing love, Rose, who describes herself as a "world-class overprotector," is trying to compensate, through her twelve-year-old daughter, Noelle, for a childhood lacking in emotional safety and physical security. Rose's father, who was mentally ill, was abusive to her mother. "I knew when the abuse was about to happen," says Rose. "When I heard my father yelling at my mother and slamming doors, I would run upstairs to their bedroom and carry on until he calmed down. I sometimes snuck in my parents' room at night and slept in their bed between them. I felt as long as I was there, there would be no fighting, no hitting."

At ten, Rose was to spend the summer with her cousins in Montpelier, Vermont. She was reluctant to go, having convinced herself that as long as she was home, she could keep her mother safe. While she was in Montpelier, her mother's appendix burst and she was rushed to the hospital for emergency surgery. "I knew I wasn't responsible for her appendix," says Rose, "but I remember feeling that if only I had been there, my mother would have been safe." This kind of thinking, which she now acknowledges as irrational, has followed her into motherhood. "I believe that if my daughter Noelle is with me, if she is in my reach, if I can see and hear her, then I can keep her safe."

To complicate matters, Rose resented her parents for having given her too much freedom and too little guidance. With both parents gone all day in their hardware store, she was left to keep herself busy and to decide what was safe and what wasn't. "When I was a teenager," she recalls, "three of my friends planned to go hiking one Saturday in the state park. Their parents all refused to let them go without a chaperone. They got so mad at their parents, but I recall being even angrier at mine, who said, 'Fine, whatever, go.' How could my parents have loved me if they never imposed rules for keeping me safe? Today, I may drive Noelle crazy with all my rules and restrictions, but at least she'll know I love her."

Indeed, Noelle may very well grow up knowing she is loved—overprotected children generally know that a great deal of love motivates their parents—but for the time being, it's hard not to notice that Noelle has fewer physical skills than her peers and low confidence. The only risks she takes are artistic ones: She paints and weaves. She still hasn't learned to swim because her fear of drowning is too great, and when the other children go sledding, she watches; the fear of pain obsesses her.

Overprotected Children

When we overprotect because we're concerned about getting children through today alive, we don't always pause to weigh the short-term or long-term negative consequences of our overprotection. If we ask, "So what if I'm being overprotective?" we're not so interested in an answer. Mostly we want to be reassured by other parents or by experts that whatever we're doing is okay, because for the life of us, we don't see alternatives. In fact, we may not find our overprotection problematic at all—we may judge, as my mother did, that any parent who doesn't overprotect as we do is "bad."

Yet overprotection does take a toll. While it may not be as easy to identify the child who suffers from overprotection as it is to identify the overprotective parent, nonetheless we might look for overprotection as a contributing factor when we observe any one of these following difficulties in a young child:

○ Inability to assess and meet one's own needs
○ Unrelenting disobedience at home and at school; tyrannical behavior, attention seeking
○ Temper tantrums, whining to get one's way
○ Refusal to eat what's been served
○ Difficulty in making friends
○ Inability to function in a group of peers
○ Bed-wetting
○ Anxiety about going to school
○ Anxiety about leaving home without a parent
○ Anxiety about being left home with a sitter
○ Over-responsiveness and over-solicitousness to a parent's needs and moods
○ Excessive worry about one's own health
○ Excessive fear about new physical challenges
○ Frustration when solving problems
○ Reluctance to express thoughts and feelings

What about the long-term consequences? What personal challenges might overprotected children like those of Frederick, Colleen, and Rose have to anticipate overcoming?

If you meet Elena, an ethereal-looking twenty-four-year-old third-grade teacher who has lived in Syracuse, New York, her entire life, you will get a sense of the kind of price a child eventually pays for having been overprotected. Elena says her parents have always worried excessively about her physical and emotional safety, far more than they worried about her brothers. In fact, and this will surprise no one, overprotective energies are focused differently on girls and boys. Many of the parents I interviewed said they overprotected their daughters because they believed they were physically more vulnerable—

more frail emotionally, more apt to be preyed upon, less capable of defending themselves. Even if parents didn't feel their own daughters were easy victims, they agreed that because women are generally seen as victims, daughters were more at risk than sons. In this same sampling, overprotection of boys was typically keyed to social and professional issues: Parents fretted about their sons falling in with a wrong crowd or not striving hard enough to become successful as adults.

Elena's situation, then, was typical: "If I were baby-sitting across the street," says Elena, "my little brother would have to watch me cross over. The boys could do what they wanted, but as a girl I couldn't. My father says, 'A girl is weaker, a girl can get hurt.'"

Elena hesitates to connect all of the overprotection she received to gender. "My brothers had different personalities. As a child, I was the kind of person who would permit my parents to hold me back. My brothers always responded to being held down by saying, 'No way, good-bye, I'm getting out.' And that's just what they did when my parents stood in their way." (One might well wonder: Was Elena, indeed, the kind of person who couldn't stand up to overprotection, or was she socialized, as a young girl, to believe that she was too frail and bound to be too compliant to resist her parents' hovering?)

Most children are good at identifying if their parents are protecting one sibling more than others, and they're quick to measure their parents' level of protection against that of other parents. According the Elena, "I knew my parents' protection was excessive because I had a constant point of comparison with our cousins, Eric and Cynthia, who lived in Henrietta. Their parents were far more liberal and allowed them more freedom. My mother distrusted outsiders, anyone outside the family. 'All you need is your family,' said my mother. 'Your friends will go and leave you.'" This reminded me of a phrase we were obliged to recite in my own family: "No friends, no fun, till you're twenty-one."

Elena was prohibited from going to sleep-over parties at friends' houses. "I could go to the party, but I'd be picked up before bedtime. No reason, so they must not have trusted me—though don't ask me what I could have done wrong in the fifth grade. In high school, my mom feared I would drink at unchaperoned parties. She'd say, 'It's not that I don't trust you; there's just so many crazies out there.' In my opinion, with my mother being so restrictive and my father alternating between being full of fun and full of unprovoked anger and meanness, we had more crazies living under our roof than I could have found in the outside world."

Just how much difficulty any child encounters because of overprotection depends upon the other stresses a child must contend with, the intensity of overprotection a child is receiving, and the child's native resiliency.

Experts on children and risk conclude that high parental anxiety is indeed a form of risk. While a high level of anxiety might be provoked by a realistic danger, such as neighborhood violence, some parents also exhibit a free-floating anxiety that is not connected to any specific or probable danger. If high parental anxiety is compounded by three or four other forms of risk to the child, such as a parent's mental illness, a family's poverty, lack of social supports for the child, or violence in the environment, research has shown that the child can suffer. For instance, a study of four-year-olds subjected to multiple forms of risk, including high parental anxiety, has demonstrated that IQ scores tend to be lower for these children.

A child's response to overprotection is further tempered by specific motivations behind his or her overprotection and by the circumstances of his or her family life: Was the child born or adopted after a long period of infertility or unsuccessful pregnancies? Was the child premature or sickly? Is the parent highly unconfident but eager for approval? Is the parent ambivalent or unhappy about the responsibilities of child care? Is the parent in a sexually or emotionally unsatisfying marriage?

If a child is eventually able to grasp a logical motivation for the overprotection, he or she is less likely to see him or herself as personally inept.

A child's ability to cope with overprotection is also tempered by the completeness of the overprotective environment. Just how intense and unyielding is the overprotection? Are both parents overprotectors, or is one either lenient in the extreme or just plain sensible? Is there an outsider enabler—a relative, older sibling, adult friend, teacher, or clergyman—who regularly offers the child an opportunity for freedoms, responsibilities, and physical and social challenges during summers or weekends? Can the enabler help give the child perspective, explaining that his parents love him and are proud of him but overprotect because they are anxious? Can the enabler help the child to negotiate with her parents for more freedom? Can the child find places outside the home where freedom, responsibilities, and opportunities for risk-taking are possible, such as in a church group, at sleep-away camp, or in boarding school? Is overprotection limited to a particular stage of development, such as infancy or adolescence, during which time a parent feels heightened anxiety? Is overprotection limited to certain activities that parents see as particularly harmful, such as co-ed activities, swimming, or driving? In these cases where the overprotection of the child isn't altogether comprehensive, the damaging consequences are mitigated.

A child's personality is one more factor that determines how much overprotection will affect him or her now and into adulthood. It is not enough to know that a child has been overprotected: We must consider how a particular child experiences that overprotection and how the child understands how it has affected his or her life. One child who notes that she is the only sibling who is overprotected might conclude that she needs greater protection because she is more fragile, clumsier, less trusted. Another child, also the lone overprotected sibling, might conclude she is dearer and better loved. When all siblings are all overprotected, as is often the case, they might conclude together that the overprotection has nothing to do with them individually; it is not an assessment of their character at all. They might decide all the fussing and restrictions just reflect their parents' anxiety gone out of control. Though the overprotection is a source of irritation and frustration, they may decide it has nothing to do with them as individuals and nothing to do with the actual dangers the world holds.

The child who is more resilient in the face of stress is better able to pull through overprotection. Numerous factors predict a child's resilience. Some factors are rooted in personality: A more resilient child typically is affectionate, confident, realistic, flexible, adaptable, self-disciplined, and able to cope with pressure and recover from disappointment. Other factors that predict resilience and help a child cope with high parental anxiety and other forms of stress are environmental: These include a secure emotional attachment with a primary caretaker and access to support and close relationships from outside the family.

When an overprotected child reaches adulthood, long-term consequences, difficult to undo, can emerge. We can see this clearly in Elena's case. Though Elena has long judged her parents' restrictiveness and high level of worry to be misguided, she has not been able to overcome all the fear instilled in her and break out, be self-reliant, or trust others. "I may be stronger now, but I'm still afraid of taking risks and making changes because I'm still convinced something bad will happen. Moving out of my parents' house to live with my girlfriend Meg was the scariest thing I ever did. Or take this fall, when I drove to Albany for an in-service seminar with some teachers from my school and stayed there for three days. My parents were very upset. I had to call when I got there and check in with them each night. The whole time I was gone, I kept having to convince myself that I really can take care of myself."

Elena is challenged by activities most people find mundane. "I don't like to sleep in a bed that's not my own or make a phone call to someone I don't know. Traveling—just to go visit relatives—used to make me sick. I couldn't go anywhere by myself for a long time. I was afraid to get my driver's license; and then when I got it, I was afraid to drive on highways and bridges, and I still have never driven in a really big city. I always fear my car will break down; I hear any little noise and I grip myself for an explosion." Elena was counseled by a supervisor at school to seek professional help for her anxiety, which she did. Today, she listens to tapes that teach her breathing techniques that help release the tension in her body. Regular aerobic exercise has helped, too; having increased her physical strength, she feels more confident about her body.

"When I moved in with Meg, I thought, Wow! I did that! Think of that! I was afraid to do it, but I did it anyway. I wish my parents could have given me some space all along, at least the space my brothers got. I wish they could have found a way to let me know I could be safe when they weren't there. I still really don't know how to make myself feel safe."

Elena's parents never encouraged her to branch out, if it meant taking risks—physical risks, emotional risks, intellectual risks. "If I did want to do something new, I couldn't tell my parents. What if one day I wanted to move away? I could never discuss any life decisions with my parents, because their fear would complicate my thinking and mix me up. I have such little confidence in myself; I know my parents' fear would steal my little courage away. Instead of telling me, 'Yes, you can do it!' or 'What's the worse that could happen?' they'll discourage me." Elena is convinced that when she most needs her parents for support and confidence, they'll only reinforce the feeling that she is too sensitive for her own good, incapable of taking care of herself.

While I am concerned to warn parents that overprotection is dangerous, I must note (and do so with a sense of personal reassurance) that people with certain personalities and certain sets of environmental or social circumstances can move beyond their overprotected childhoods (but bear in mind, it isn't easy—and imagine how that energy might be better used!) Loretta, a lawyer and mother of two, insists her innate personality permitted her to resist and overcome the ill effects of overprotection. "I should have become as cautious and fearful as my siblings," says Loretta, "but it didn't happen."

How could this be? From an early age, Loretta rejected her parents' view of the world and created a romantic image for herself: "I was the dragon slayer, the risk taker who marched off into experience unafraid. This was possible because the family norms were so confining, so constraining, so constricting. With so much forbidden, any risk I took seemed rash, bold, and daring. I badly needed to defy my parents."

"My parents took note of my adventurous nature: I wanted to go abroad, have torrid love affairs, ride horses, learn to fly. This made them all the more nervous for me. One summer, I rescued a boyfriend after he jumped off the boat we were sailing and got a cramp in his leg. The newspaper reporter who covered the rescue called me a hero. According to my mother, however, I had foolishly risked my life. She said, 'Of all of my children, only Loretta would get into this kind of trouble.' This rescue was the kind of thing my parents dreaded, the kind of thing they knew I would do."

While Loretta is proud of her resistance and sees it as heroic, her bitterness lingers; she remains angry that she has needed to expend so much energy continually fashioning herself into a courageous person.

Siblings Resist Overprotection

Kevin, a fifty-year-old engineer, speculates that he was able to emerge from an overprotected childhood fairly intact because of a number of factors that are less reflective of personality and more reflective of the situation he was in. "First of all," says Kevin, "the overprotection I received was limited in scope, and only certain behaviors caused my parents, second-generation Irish Catholics, to fret in high gear. For the most part, they worried about the very same things that every other parent worried about: falling and breaking bones, putting things into eyeballs, getting in front of moving vehicles, running around with sharp objects. But there were two taboos that sent them over the edge, and when it came to those, they overprotected. The first taboo was swimming, and that was because my father's brother drowned as a child after diving into shallow water. Consequently, we were permitted to go only to a municipal pool that was three feet at the deepest point. Even there, the older children had to watch the younger ones constantly. We were never taught to swim. Today, I would never go in water over my head."

The second issue that put Kevin's parents into a protective frenzy was their fear of teenage pregnancy. "My mother got pregnant when she was a teenager. She never talked about it; I'm not even sure how we all knew, but we did, and we knew not to breathe a word. Because of her own experience, my mother viewed our teen years as being particularly treacherous. The Catholic Church, in part, was her answer, since Church doctrine prohibited intercourse outside of wedlock. My father indicated that there was a shotgun in his closet and it was kept clean and ready."

Kevin's sisters grew up terrified they would get pregnant even if they didn't have sex; the brothers grew up fearing they'd end up getting shot by some girl's father. Kevin's oldest sister never dated in high school, though not from lack of opportunity. "Nanette was beautiful and popular. One night, just after she had graduated high school and had started working, she was walked home on a summer evening by a young man. My mother watched from the second-floor window. When my sister came through the front door, my mother ran down, grabbed her by the hair, and pulled her up the stairs, cursing her all the way, telling her she was filth. The rest of us watched, the sisters watching harder. None of the sisters ever got pregnant before marriage, and none of the boys got anyone pregnant. Nanette ended up with severe psychological problems and was hospitalized for long periods. Were her subsequent problems related to our mother's obsession with unwanted pregnancies? I never knew, but I always felt it stood to reason that there was some connection."

Kevin credits a second factor for his emergence from overprotection, and that was having five other siblings who could band together and strategize to circumvent parental authority. When it came to dating, which clearly raised parental anxiety sky-high, Kevin and his siblings learned to lie and cover for each other. Rebelling collectively, they stretched the short leash they were held on until it broke. Often they'd discuss why their parents protected as they did, and in talking about it amongst themselves, they were able to make sense of it and release some of their anger.

Overprotected Children, Overprotective Parents

Frequently and unfortunately, the child who is overprotected often grows up to become the parent who overprotects. Researchers at the University of Texas at Austin have demonstrated that "caregivers who were overprotected during childhood are likely to view the world as a dangerous place where others cannot be trusted."

Meet Mark, a thirty-four-year-old chemist who is the overprotected child of Hungarian Holocaust survivors who had emigrated to the United States. He is also the overprotective father of twin four-year-old boys.

When Mark applied to college, his parents told him he could go anywhere. He had read about Stanford and wanted to go there, but when he was accepted, his parents said, "All the way to California? That's too far away! What if you got sick? Where would you be then? Who would look out for you? You would be all alone. You were accepted to the University of Chicago and Northwestern. Pick one of those and stay here in Chicago." And so Mark went to the University of Chicago, wondering if his parents wanted him to stay near home to protect him or to protect themselves.

If Mark once felt as though he wore an invisible tether, he still feels that way. "I'm still in Chicago. I went to college here, graduate school here, I work here, I'm raising my own family here. At each juncture, I've had opportunities to move away, but I always justified staying. Now I tell myself I can't move away because I have elderly parents to look after."

Mark was able to have adventures growing up, but each adventure required him to overcome anxiety and trepidation. "I forced myself to go hiking in the Rockies even though I'm terrified of heights. While hiking, I'd count the moments until I was safe at home. Actually, the best part of the adventure was imagining how good it would be to be home again. Once my friend Seth and I were climbing over a high pass and there was a tremendous thunderstorm with lightning striking all around. I was praying to God and hunched over, running. I pictured myself laid out, dead. Seth laughed at me. 'Why are you laughing?' I asked. 'Aren't you also afraid we'll get killed?' Seth said, 'So we'll get killed.'"

"When I returned home, my father said, 'You were gone for two weeks! I thought after a day or two you'd give up and come back home.' My mother, who also carries memories of the war as well as memories of an impoverished childhood, is even more concerned than my father about eating, sleeping, being physically comfortable. When I used to complain that the TV was always on in our house, my mother would respond, 'What's wrong with relaxing on occasion?' No matter what I was doing, even if I wasn't studying, she always nudged me to stop working so hard and relax. If TV was on, and I was sitting there on the couch between my parents watching, then she knew I was safe and accounted for. On the surface, my parents claimed they wanted me to succeed and accomplish things: They said they wanted me to go out and make the most of my life and be free to do whatever I wanted. But that's not what they really wanted. Their true desire was to have me right there, safe, relaxing, in place, not too far off."

How are these childhood experiences reflected in Mark's attitude toward his own sons? Mark finds himself reproducing his parents' overprotection, even though he has been limited and pained by it. The habits of outlandish worry have become so engrained that when Mark and his wife reluctantly appeared at his company's annual, lavish holiday banquet, all Mark could think about was the boys, even though he knew they were being well cared for at home by his mother-in-law. "A free-floating anxiety has grown on me since I became a parent, almost an appendage. I have gotten so used to worrying about the boys, I have forgotten how not to worry. When I'm at work, I'm always worrying that something terrible has happened. I imagine Jordan running head-on into the fireplace, Darren pulling a pot off the stove and burning himself. I have this nightmare of my wife falling and getting hurt and not being able to do anything and the boys being upset and crying. Jordan did once run into the fireplace and gashed the side of his head. I keep reliving the scene: his blood gushing, wrapping him up in towels, running him to the emergency ward."

Mark's long list of fears extends into the boys' future. "To-night, when I put the boys to bed, Jordan was afraid of monsters, then he gave the idea to Darren. I couldn't leave them until they were asleep. I wondered, one day the boys will come to me and say, 'I'm afraid of dying.' What will I tell them? What if they grow up with a bottomless, lonely feeling that no one loves them? Or if they want something badly and they try to get it and fail. How will I comfort them when they discover they can't be the best at something, when their girl-friends drop them? I'm always feeling as if I've failed them already, or will fail them soon enough."

Mark would acknowledge that he has not made much effort

to learn to parent differently. But even when the recipient of overprotection has consciously tried to parent differently, overprotective attitudes still sneak up. Consider the case of Erika, a forty-six-year-old town council woman. Erika's parents, who overprotected her, instilled in her a sense that the world was not a safe place and that no one can be trusted except for family. Coming from this kind of background, Erika made an effort to encourage her own daughter, now nineteen, and her son, now twenty-one, to be independent and capable. "My heart was in my throat always, but I let them climb to the highest point of the jungle gym and dive off the highest diving board at age five. When the time came for them to leave home and go to university, I assumed I would be prepared. But the reality of my first child leaving hit me harder than I ever could have imagined. I became anxious, depressed, controlling. I needed to hear every detail of his plans and nothing seemed thought through enough to me. My fear had taken over; that part of me that could once hold my heart in my throat no longer functioned."

How can we actively keep ourselves from raising children who will be pained and limited by our overprotection—even when we're trying to take active measures not to overprotect? We begin by learning to better understand our own fears and where they come from and evaluating the dangers our children face. Many think of this as "drawing the thin line between protection and overprotection."

4

Drawing the Thin Line Between
Protection and Overprotection

The process of learning to release children into the world at the right times and places starts from the very beginning.

It is risky, deadly even, to rein our children in until young adulthood and then, poof, release them to the world. "Our son Jeff was a walking target," says Regina, "stick-thin and gangly as a string bean." Regina and her husband, Leland, protected Jeff from danger by restricting where he could go, even through college. It didn't dawn on them to help Jeff pick up street smarts or to help him discover how he might project less physical vulnerability. When he was twenty-two years old and went to dental school at the University of Pennsylvania in downtown Philadelphia, his ignorance and naiveté caught up with him. Jeff and his classmate Paul went out to a local pizza place after a late night of studying. An argument broke out between two other customers. "Jeff and Paul didn't understand that an argument could be anything more than an exchange of words or a punch in the nose," says Regina. "Guns came out, and the boys watched to see what would happen next, as if they were spectators at Universal Studios. They didn't duck, they didn't take cover. Paul was killed in the crossfire."

Jeff's classmates then took him under their wing and gave

him a crash course in self-protection. They told him he had to be aware of where he was going, what he was doing, and how he was acting. They showed him how his body language telegraphed his vulnerability, and they encouraged him to work out. Most important, they put Jeff through hypothetical scenarios: What would you do if . . . ? This way he'd know what options he had for reacting, having rehearsed them mentally. One morning, when Jeff was dressed in his hospital whites and was on his way to the clinic, he was mugged by two teenage boys. Having considered this scenario beforehand, Jeff knew he could take on one teenager but not two. As he had rehearsed, he did not yell "Help!" as his friends had told him passersby are reluctant to get involved if they think they'll be exposed to violence. Jeff began yelling incoherently, as if he were having a seizure, and people rushed to his aid. When they arrived, the teenagers fled.

Jeff was lucky not to have been shot, lucky to have fallen in with caring, savvy friends. Our own overprotected children shouldn't have to rely on luck. Their childhood training should prepare them to discriminate between what's safe and what's not, and help them to be able to recognize and cope with danger.

Holding and Releasing

How do we know when to hold on and when to let go?

It seems so complicated. That's because every decision we make for our children can feel as if it has life-and-death consequences. Though we can estimate what those consequences may be, we can never predict what will happen with 100-percent accuracy. The slightest margin of doubt can send us spinning.

Protection is not an all-or-nothing process. As I have suggested, at each stage of our children's development, we alternate between finding the right times to hold on and the right times to let them go, measuring our hold and release like the footwork we perform as we drive our cars, almost intuitively switching from gas pedal to brake and then back to gas, as the situation demands. (Yes—we do occasionally have to slam on the brakes!) Of course, at each stage of development, issues differ dramatically: During a child's infancy, we debate whether we can safely let our baby cry just a few moments before we rush in to see if he's okay; during the teenage years, we debate whether we will give our daughter our blessings when she announces she and her friends would like to go hiking along the Appalachian Trail.

Whatever stage of the game we and our children are at, we need to see how our own fear influences how we protect. We need to distinguish between fear that alerts us to danger and fear that is better quieted or swallowed for the sake of our children's well-being.

There is no foolproof recipe for making these complex protective decisions. One nine-year-old might be allowed to use the oven to prepare a soup-to-nuts dinner for the family, but for another nine-year-old, this might be deadly. And while all teenagers are allowed to obtain learner's permits at the same age in each state, we know all teenagers are not equally ready —and neither are their parents.

While there are no simple or clear-cut solutions that work in every case for every child, there are still general strategies we can turn to for help as we draw that thin line between protection and overprotection.

What's Safe? What's Not?
Green Light, Red Light, Yellow Light

The Green Light—When It's Okay to Let Go
Keeping children *perfectly* safe, physically and emotionally, is not a realistic goal. If it were, we'd consume ourselves with anxiety and guilt.

But if we can determine that the chance of something going wrong for a child is really minimal, it is both wise and realistic for us to decide that we can let go. We make that decision after consideration, research, and discussion. I've come to think of the protective situations that indicate we can let go as the *green lights*. There are three kinds of green-light situations: those that are easy to work through, those that are more challenging, and those that are truly difficult.

Easy Green: Let's start with the easy green-light situations. Say your in-laws, healthy, dependable, and comfortable with children, offer to babysit for your young children while you go to the movies in town. You may feel that you've made the decision to accept their offer without any thought, but in fact you probably weighed a number of factors in the seconds before concluding that this was a green light. You probably asked yourself and answered the following questions:

Q: How capable are my in-laws?
A: Utterly trustworthy.

Q: Am I sure?
A: Of course!

Q: What evidence do I have?
A: They've baby-sat before and have done just fine. Besides, the kids look forward to their coming and won't put up a fuss when we leave.

Q: What's the very worst thing that could possibly and realistically happen here?
A: The kids could refuse to go to sleep.

Q: If that happens, would it be so bad?
A: No. The in-laws would be forgiving, and the children will nap tomorrow.

Q: Could I be reached in the case of a major emergency?
A: Absolutely. I can leave a phone number and get back quickly.

The questions you ask yourself are simple and clear-cut and so are the answers. It's unlikely that you need to investigate further or consult with anyone. You know you can easily take any emergency precautions—leaving a number where you can be reached and the numbers of a neighbor and the pediatrician. If something does go wrong, the consequences aren't too serious.

At each stage of a child's life, there will be many protective situations in which you might readily decide, green light—let go! Here are some examples that may arise at each stage of development:

Pregnancy and infancy: *Can you keep exercising while you're pregnant if you're doing fine? Can you take an infant out on a nice day? Can you take the baby on an airplane?*

Toddlers and preschoolers: *Can you enroll your child in nursery school? Is it okay for the child to begin having a variety of appropriate grown-up foods?*

School-age children: *Can your child go to a friend's house to play, pick out his own clothes, or help out in the kitchen?*

Teenagers: *Can your child stay after school for clubs, babysit, or do yard work for other families?*

Challenging Green: Challenging green-light situations require more consideration before they are resolved. Perhaps you have a newborn baby and wonder, "Can I let him lie in his crib while I take a shower, or does someone always have to be on guard?" If the answer isn't readily apparent as you begin to evaluate the situation, you might need to turn to a more experienced parent or child-care expert, such as a nurse or pediatrician, who will probably reassure you: "You know your baby can't get out of the crib. You know you can take every necessary precaution—checking to see that no pillows, blankets, or bumpers can interfere with your baby's breathing; making sure no family pets or curious older siblings can leap into the crib or knock it down." Once you've digested the information you hear or have culled from books, and once you have taken the appropriate precautions, you'll have the confidence to leave a baby alone while you shower.

The following developmental stages carry their own challenging green-light situations:

> Pregnancy and infancy: *Should you take the vitamins your obstetrician is prescribing? Should your baby have all the new inoculations that are being recommended? Can you take the baby out on a snowy day?*
>
> Toddlers and preschoolers: *Can your child begin to select the foods she prefers? Can your child play in a fenced backyard area without constant supervision?*
>
> School-age children: *Can your child walk home from the nearby bus stop alone? Can your child prepare his own easy breakfasts?*
>
> Teenagers: *Can your child get a learner's permit and learn to drive? Can she go downtown with friends?*

Difficult Green: Some green-light decisions are truly difficult to work through, even when they clearly do not involve life-or-death situations. You'll have reservations that keep you ruminating, even after you've given the situation serious consideration. You may have many remaining questions that are not easily or definitively answered by books or experts. You may need to look for input from numerous sources—from your child, your partner, your parents, your siblings, your friends, your children's teachers, your pediatricians and nurses. You may need to observe your child at length in a variety of situations in order to assess his or her readiness and needs before you can give the go-ahead. You may need to think a great deal about how your child's current situation evokes memories of your own past and arouses your insecurities. You may have to be prepared to take complicated precautions and acknowledge that emergencies could come up. After all this, even if you don't feel completely at peace, you may still conclude that's it's best to go ahead and decide that yes, this is safe enough—it's a green light.

Here's an example of one such difficult green-light decision. Say your teenage son, a good student but not a math wiz, wants to know if you'll allow him to sign up for a very difficult AP calculus course. His guidance counselor and math teacher are all for it. Surely he can do it, they say, if he really applies himself. But you're not so ready to give the go-ahead.

You can't help hearing the iffiness in his voice. Is he trying to say "I don't know if I can do this" or "I really don't want to do this, and I need you to help me get out of it"? On top of playing basketball and writing for the newspaper, would AP calculus be just enough pressure to push him over the edge? You're not worried about a nervous breakdown, but with all the talk about drugs and teenage suicide, you worry about imposing unnecessary stress. What's the hurry? He can take calculus in college.

The difficult green-light situations typically send you back to memories of your own childhood experiences. Perhaps you'll recall a course you took that was way over your head and the resulting pressure that ruined senior year. On the other hand, you may acknowledge that just because you once succumbed to pressure, it doesn't mean your son will repeat your experience.

You may recognize how anxious you get to see your child stressed and under pressure, how upset you get if you feel powerless to help. But you may ultimately acknowledge that just because you feel inadequate to meet the challenge of your child's stress, that's no reason he should lower his horizons. If you advise your son against the course, he may think you have no faith in him—and, goodness, that's not the case at all.

You realize that you haven't been listening to your son thus far. What does he want, fear, or expect? At first all he says is, "I dunno. That's why I asked you." Not much help. But as an aside, he mentions, "Tom, Adam, and Noah are all taking AP." This does help. You don't want him to feel left out of an experience his best buddies, all his intellectual equals, will have. Since the boys will have each other to tough it out together, you finally decide to encourage your son to take the course. Finally, the decision is clear: Alas, a green light!

In these difficult green-light situations, the deliberations can grow so unwieldy that we forget how well we can generally intuit what's right for a child. But once we get a grip on ourselves, look at the situation from different angles, and locate truly important reasons for letting go, we can decide it's okay. Here are some examples of truly challenging green-light situations:

Pregnancy and infancy: *Can you deliver your baby at home with a midwife in attendance? Can the baby begin full-time day care or be cared for all day by a new nanny?*

Toddlers and preschoolers: *Do you act on your doctor's recommendation that the child have her tonsils out or have tubes put in her ears?*

School-age children: *Can you let a child who's older than ten stay home alone for short periods of time? Do you let your child know that a grandparent is terminally ill?*

Teenagers: *Will you permit your child to drive at night? If your child has asked for contraceptives, will you help him or her to get them?*

Red Light

Just as some protective situations will set off a green light and permit us to release our children, others will set off a red light, and we will conclude that it's too risky to let go. The red light means we hold on, at least for the time being. Situations that set off a red light come in the same three varieties: some are easy to work through, some are more challenging, and some are truly difficult.

Easy Red: Most parents can readily identify the easy red light situations and work them through quickly. You know the situation is not safe for any child, or for your child in particular, and the answer is "No way!" or "Not yet!" The easy red-light decisions feel as if they come to us in an instant, but of course we have given them some thought.

Here's an example of an easy red light: You receive a baby walker as a shower present from your sister. But you've read in parenting magazines that walkers are unsafe, and the pediatrician you've interviewed has warned you against them. You trust that what you've read and heard is true: Babies left unattended in walkers have fallen down staircases and have ended up in emergency rooms with concussions and bruises. No thank you. Though it may hurt your sister's feelings (though she chides, "Both my children used walkers safely and loved them. Boy, you haven't even given birth and you're already being overprotective!"), you take the flack and exchange the walker for a different piece of baby equipment.

It's simple to respond to easy red-light situations such as this. You have concrete evidence from experts you respect that something will not be safe for your child and nothing anyone says otherwise dissuades you. The risks, you know, far outweigh any advantages. You feel secure your fears are rooted in reality. Even if you're accused of being overprotective, you won't budge and that's final!

Here are some examples of the easy red-light situations that might occur during each stage of childhood development:

Pregnancy and infancy: *Can you drink or smoke while pregnant? Can your child ride in a car without a car seat?*

Toddlers and preschoolers: *Can you read a magazine while your child wades in the baby pool?*

School-age children: *Can your child ride a bike even though she's lost her helmet?*

Teenagers: *Can your teen be driven home by friends after the prom?*

Challenging Red Light: Red-light situations that are more challenging require more thought on our parts. The impulse to say no might well up in us immediately, but before we issue our decision, we need to struggle to understand why we feel so strongly and analyze if we are using good judgment. Finally, if most other families are seeing a green light in the very same situation in which we see a red light, we have to ask if we're really right about our decision and right about sticking to it.

I have a personal example of a challenging red-light decision that I made for my first child even before she was born. I was living in Germany, and my obstetrician offered me the drug Bendectin to combat nausea in pregnancy. While I hated feeling nauseous and was losing weight, I wondered if this drug was as safe as the doctor claimed. Two other pregnant women I knew weren't worried at all about taking the drug. I still wasn't so sure, and living abroad, I didn't have easy access to medical literature. As I continued to deliberate, I recalled a friend from college who learned she was at risk for cancer because her mother had been given the drug DES in pregnancy. When I finally decided not to take the Bendectin, the only hard evidence I had to go on was the misery of a friend who was a "DES daughter." Hardly scientific, I admit, but I concluded that I would rather be nauseous than court risk. Conclusive evidence connecting Bendectin to birth defects is still not in, but every time I read about a mother who once took Bendectin who is now convinced that it caused her child's birth defects, I feel that I made a good choice.

Over the years, I have remained leery about giving my children medication doctors describe as "optional." One of my daughters had febrile seizures when she was a toddler, a generally nonthreatening situation that usually clears up with time. A specialist I consulted told me I could give her phenobarbital.

(As it turns out, recent research claims that phenobarbital may sedate children, making them lethargic, even lowering their IQ scores. This drug, now considered minimally effective for febrile seizures, has been replaced with Valium.) Should I protect my child from having seizures, as the doctor was suggesting, or should I protect my child from the phenobarbital? I sorted out the facts I had. My doctor had said the seizures were not dangerous to children, though they were terrifying to the parent who watched. The seizures certainly frightened me, but should I drug my child to avoid a stressful situation for myself? As the doctor was giving me a choice, I decided, for the time being, to give the medicine a red light. If the seizures were infrequent and not dangerous, and moreover would probably be outgrown, why give a little child such a potent drug? If the situation changed, I could reconsider.

These are examples of challenging red-light decisions we might expect to face:

Pregnancy and infancy: *If your pediatrician says your child's speech delay is nothing to be concerned about, but you have a strong feeling something is not quite right, should you ignore her optimism and seek out the advice of specialists?*

Toddlers and preschoolers: *If your in-laws or parents visit frequently and bring the children sweets or expensive gifts you don't approve of, can you tell them their offerings are inappropriate, even if their feelings might be hurt?*

School-age children: *If your child claims other kids are going to see a movie that you think contains horrifying violence or explicit sexuality that you think is harmful for a youngster, will you still permit him to go?*

Teenagers: *Can your child go on a white-water canoeing trip with a neighbor who claims he is capable of supervising seven teenagers alone?*

Difficult Red: What makes the most difficult red-light decision so trying is our sense of powerlessness. These are decisions our children will make without consulting us or decisions they must make for themselves. We may be certain that the right response is to say "No way" or "Not yet," but in these situations, we know the decision isn't really ours to make. We can give our child input and hopefully set the stage for good decision-making, but ultimately the child will have to make the choice alone and cope with the consequences.

Here's an example. Gordon's seventeen-year-old son Mitch had gotten his driver's license and had worked all year after school in a diner to buy an old car for tooling around town. Gordon was proud of Mitch, who tended to abandon the projects he started. In June, after purchasing an old VW, Mitch announced that he and some friends wanted to drive cross-country and get summer jobs in California. It sounded crazy to Gordon. "The car was a heap of junk. It would have been fine for driving around town, but there was no way it would make it to California. Mitch was not an experienced driver and there was all that life out there for him to deal with. But Mitch is a willful and headstrong boy. The surest way to convince him he had to go to California, no matter what I said, was to tell him he couldn't go. He had worked hard to get the car; maybe what had motivated all of his work was this dream of going far away, a dream he didn't dare tell me about."

Calmly, Gordon said to his son, "Okay, let's talk about it. Who will you go with? What will you do if the car breaks down? Who will you stay with? What kind of job will you get?" After talking at length, Mitch decided too many things could go wrong that he wasn't prepared to handle. "He decided he wasn't ready. But he wanted to see if I would have trusted him enough to let him go, and he saw that I had. When he graduated college and had many driving adventures under his belt, he told me that he was grateful I hadn't forbidden him to go cross-country at seventeen: 'I didn't have to go off and do it just to prove to you that you couldn't forbid me from doing something.' "

The following are examples of these most difficult red-light decisions, which obviously come up only with older children:

> School-age children: *Can your child hang out with a group of kids who seem like a bunch of mischief makers?*
> Teenagers: *Can your child get engaged? get married? drop out of school? go to a party where there will be drinking?*

Yellow Lights

Finally, there are the yellow lights, protective decisions that shout out to us "Be careful! Be careful!" Yellow lights are tricky, for even after we've asked all the questions, done all the research, observed and queried our children, consulted all sources of advice and wisdom, considered our gut reactions, considered the precautions that could be taken, and considered the consequences, we're still left scratching our heads. Yellow lights gnaw at us, because for the time being, we still don't know what to do, and we find ourselves in limbo, hovering between holding on and letting go. With yellow lights, we don't so much decide as postpone deciding. We can only hope that in time we'll know better what to do. If we don't have the luxury of time and have to guess, we can only hope we've guessed well.

The yellow-light situation I and so many other parents are wrestling with these days concerns Lyme disease, which is spread by ticks carried by deer. Six years ago, my husband and I bought a house on the edge of the woods so we and the children could go adventuring. But there are deer all over our woods, and they've even invaded the garden and graze on our flowers. Each year, more neighbors have contracted Lyme disease. In next town over, residents are holding fund-raisers for a family that can no longer pay to treat a daughter who has been debilitated by Lyme disease. I'm convinced this is a real problem we're facing and not just a looming threat. But what am I supposed to do? Refuse to let my girls play in the woods? Some of my neighbors won't let their children venture beyond their screened porches. I don't have the heart to do that, at least not yet. For the time being, I still allow the girls to go into the woods, provided they wear long sleeves, pants, socks pulled over their pants, hats, and insect repellent. They must shower and shampoo immediately after their return and check themselves. I double-check their checking. So far, so good, but I worry that I'm still being cavalier. Once, a situation arose that intensified my concern and my doubts about the precautionary measures we're taking: My pediatrician advised me that if my daughter's flulike symptoms didn't clear up in two days, she'd better come in for the blood work for Lyme disease. Oh my God, I thought, and literally began to tremble, because I know how devastating Lyme disease can be and felt guilty I had not done enough to prevent it. What was I thinking? That I could wish the ticks away?

It was a flu. That time. For me, deciding what to do about Lyme disease isn't just a hard call—it's an impossible one, and that's what yellow-light situations are all about. For the time being, I'm stumped. I hear myself not encouraging the girls to play in the woods as often as I once did. I can only hope that in time I'll know better what to do and that the girls will remain safe.

Here are some other yellow-light situations currently stumping parents:

> **Pregnancy and infancy:** *Should you take all the tests to detect fetal abnormalities that obstetricians are now advising? Should you extend your maternity/paternity leave if some experts are now saying that babies don't flourish as well in day care?*
>
> **Toddlers and preschoolers:** *If your toddler still enjoys nursing,*

do you still have to wean him? If your child is having a lot of trouble separating from you, should you give in and stay home rather than go out for the evening?

School-age children: *Will your child be safer if you enroll him in a private, parochial, or single-sex school, even if that means limiting social and intellectual horizons? Can you let your child go off with your ex on weekends, even though you think he or she is a crummy parent?*

Teenagers: *If you suggest your child get contraceptives, will you inadvertently be sanctioning sexual activity? Can you permit your child to play football, given all you hear about injuries?*

Evaluate, Evaluate, Evaluate

Each time we make a decision about protecting a child, no matter how old the child is, no matter if the situation is a green light, red light, or yellow light, we engage in a process of evaluation. Except in the simplest situations, it is rarely an easy process to draw the thin line between what's safe and what's not. If it's any consolation, the more accustomed we get to the process of evaluation, the more automatically we're able to work our way through situations without becoming overwhelmed. Most of us work through protective situations in a helter-skelter fashion. If, however, we work through them more systematically, we can increase our feeling of control, being confident that we have left no stone unturned.

Here, then, are some general guidelines, applicable to parents of children of all ages, for evaluating a protective situation.

Guidelines for Evaluating a
Protective Situation

Where Will It Take Place?

1. If the situation will take place inside your home, what dangers must be contended with? What changes can you make to promote greater safety?
2. If the situation takes place outside your home, what potential dangers might be encountered?
   - Does the safety of the environment change at different times of day? (A bus terminal that's creepy at night may be safe enough for a confident, well-rehearsed child during the morning and evening rush hours. A school bus stop that's generally safe may be unsafe when the mornings or afternoons get darker and visibility is limited.)
   - Who else will be in the environment at the same time? Families or young people on class trips? Commuters? Transients?
   - If you can't rely upon a firsthand evaluation of the environment, what do others whom you trust and have concrete experience say about it? What kind of a reputation does this place have? Do the stories you're told sound reliable or alarmist? (If, for example, you hear that someone was once mugged in a certain park, is it logical to assume the park is dangerous and off-limits? On the other hand, consistent problems in the recent past might be a cause for high caution. A park in which muggings take place all the time sounds like a bad bet.)
   - How might your own child, given his or her personality, flourish in this environment?

Who Will Be There to Supervise or Help?

1. You? How attentive will you be able to be at that time?

2. Other parents, teachers, older siblings, relatives, youth leaders? How much confidence do you have in their attentiveness and decision-making ability? If, for instance, parents are chaperoning a party, will they be there the *entire* time? If a big sister is the chaperone, can she be counted on to take her job seriously? If the situation poses dangers—say, as a swimming party for a group of eight-year-olds would—are the host parents sufficiently safety-conscious to remain present and have first-aid equipment on hand?

3. Professional supervision? Can you count on it? Will police officers be on board every train? Will the rock concert have enough security guards?

What Might Be the Emotional Consequences for Your Child?

How important is it that your child be able to confront this situation at this time in his life? What hinges on it? Will the decision make all the difference in the world to your child?

Is this a task he, himself, has expressed an interest in accomplishing? How important does your child say this is to him? Do you agree with his evaluation? Does he want to do it or are his peers or siblings pressuring him?

Will there be positive consequences for your child if he can say "I did it!"—a feeling of being capable or of being one of the gang?

What might the negative consequences be if he is told the situation is not safe enough or that he isn't ready? Devastation or disappointment? Anger at you or loss of self-esteem?

If nearly every child in the peer group is permitted to go, for instance, to the movies together on Saturday night, what social consequences might your child face if he cannot? Will he lose face among his peers?

Is the potential of danger so great that it will justify any ostracism your child might face? Will the situation be a little scary (like going to school on the first day) or out-and-out terrifying?

Your Child's Skills

What physical and emotional skills should your child have to be able to meet the challenges of this situation? If you decide your child is not ready, which skills are necessary for her to demonstrate her readiness and preparation in the future?

Does your child have these necessary skills securely under her belt, or is she still iffy about them? (If, for example, your daughter would like to go canoeing with friends, can she confidently keep afloat in deep water for at least five minutes? If she just learned how to tread water in camp last week, she may have the necessary skills but they may be too new to be trusted.)

If she's going to do something alone—such as cooking a meal using the stove—has she performed the task successfully numerous times when you supervised? Have you talked about all the safety precautions she should keep in mind? If she's cooking, for instance, can she put out an oven fire? Has she accomplished the task she wishes to perform enough times when you weren't watching but were nearby enough to peek in if there were questions or catastrophes? If something goes wrong, will she be even-tempered in the face of the unexpected?

Are you child's peers able to handle this and even more sophisticated challenges?

Is there some good reason that your child lags behind peers? Is he particularly fearful or prone to nightmares? Does some past frightening experience make him less able to cope with similar new experiences?

Can you count on your child to follow the safety precautions she knows if there's peer pressure to go against the rules? (For example, if her friends say a life jacket is a nerdy thing to wear, will she keep hers on or will she take it off?)

In the event that something goes wrong or changes unexpectedly, do you feel confident that your child has the ability to act calmly, safely, and resourcefully in familiar and unfamiliar situations? What has she demonstrated in the past that proves her readiness? Can your child detect danger and take steps to avoid mishap? Is your child a good enough judge of character so she can approach the right kind of person for help?

Has she been prepared to think through what could go awry and rehearse how she might react?

Will she be able to improvise if the situation changes?

Will she know how to get help if she needs it? Can you or a neighbor be available to advise or save the day, if necessary?

Imagining Worst-Case Scenarios

What is the worst thing that could go wrong, with any likelihood, in this situation? (Be reasonable here. A terrorist, for example, could enter your local Friendly's restaurant and take hostages, but it isn't likely enough to happen to merit consideration.)

If something were to go wrong, would it be the worst thing in the world? Would the consequences be unendurable for your child? (Your son, for instance, could break his finger playing basketball, but it would not be the worst thing in the world if he had his finger in a splint for a few weeks. If, on the other hand, he was about to debut on the violin in Carnegie Hall, a finger broken playing basketball could turn out to be quite the catastrophe).

How great is the probability that the worst-case scenario could happen? (For instance, the worst thing that could happen in the food court of a mall is that your baby could be abducted if you left her stroller unattended as you made your purchases. It doesn't happen all the time, but it is a terrible thing that does happen often enough to merit precautions. On the other hand, the worst thing that could probably happen if your five-year-old went on his first sleepover is that he might get very homesick and want to come home at 11:00 at night. While the probability of that happening is pretty high, the problem can easily be resolved by coming to get your little boy and assuring him he can try a sleepover again when he feels ready.)

How would you weigh the pluses against the minuses? For instance, while it is true that school children going with their classes to see Broadway plays have been pickpocketed, would that be sufficient justification for you to prohibit your own seventh grader from going with the rest of the junior high to see *Les Mis*? Probably not. If, however, you noted that the worst thing that could happen to high-school students on prom night is that they get killed by drunken young drivers, you and the other parents of seniors might decide that the risk is too great to take, and you will go all out to stage an alternative, adult-chaperoned "night to remember."

Examining Your Own Fears and Concerns

What about the whole situation makes you most afraid or leery? Can you move beyond "I get bad vibes" to the specifics?

In order to tease apart your real fears from your irrational ones, can you name what, realistically, could go wrong or do you just have a free-floating, foreboding feeling? When you picture your child in the situation, can you discover if one particular aspect of it makes you most anxious? Can you isolate which part of the scenario concerns you most and focus on that?

If a situation has unpleasant consequences, could *you* deal with them: If you permit your child to go skiing and she comes back with a broken leg (which could easily happen) or if you permit her to go camping and she comes back covered with poison ivy, can you cope with these very natural consequences without making your child feel inept or guilty?

If you believe your child is ready to meet the challenge but you're still not, can you name what, exactly, is holding you back and making you so anxious? If nearly all the other parents in your circle are willing to have their little children attend the local nursery school or have their older children go off on a religious retreat and you're not, what exactly are your reasons? Do you think that having just a little more time to get used to the idea or having some more information at hand might make all the difference? Would you feel better if you linked up with other parents whose children have met the challenge or will face it along with your child?

Does an activity clash against your values so strongly that you will prohibit it, no matter what?

Are there safety considerations you're aware of that the others are not paying attention to? Do you have special scientific knowledge or ethical concerns that cause you to make different decisions?

Do you believe your child is genuinely more fragile and needs more protection that his peers? Say you were correct in your estimation: Have you investigated other ways your child can still experience risks and freedom, given the real limitations your child works under?

With more time to get used to the idea and make enough inquiries, might you be able to let go? Would you be more comfortable if your child were just a little older or if you accompanied him on a dry run?

What would your own parents have done in this same situation when you were a child? Do you recall how you felt about their decision? Do you now agree with their judgment call?

Does this situation simply make you feel anxious for reasons that have little to do with your child but everything to do with yourself? One father, for instance, explained that while his own children have never fallen down the stairs and are fairly cautious around stairs, he lives in terror that they might one day fall and be badly injured. Why? He recalls falling down his own staircase as a child and being rushed off to the emergency room for stitches by his frantic parents. For some parents, it is easy to recall and single out the various events and attitudes in their pasts that cause them to be especially fearful as parents and to overprotect. For others, it is enough to recognize that their own life experiences are standing in the way of allowing them to give their children the autonomy they need to grow up and become competent.

According to Dr. Michelle Friedman, assistant clinical professor of psychiatry at Mount Sinai School of Medicine, old "baggage" we drag around diminishes our pleasure in the present. Even if a mental "spring cleaning" of the life experiences that stand in our way won't banish our fears forever, it helps put "red flags" in place, so we will notice when an aspect of parenting triggers a familiar feeling, such as a recurrent anxiety, despair, or obsessive worry. This is when we need to say to ourselves, "Here I am again, worrying about the same old thing." Having done that, we can attend to the real challenges our children currently face.

But it's not always possible for a parent to say, "Now that I recall being abandoned or fretted about as a child, I can stop overprotecting my own children." Such memories can be too deep and hidden for us to pull up ourselves. To usefully recall the past, or to consciously direct ourselves to replace ineffective behaviors with more effective ones, some parents will choose to turn to skilled therapists to understand what memories govern their current behaviors and to acquire conscious control over them.

Evaluating Where You Stand in Relation to Other Parents and to Your Partner

How are other parents handling the same situation? (In animal biology, this is referred to as "variations in parental solicitude.") Many parents are best able to answer the question "Am I being overprotective in general or overprotective in this particular situation?" when they compare themselves to other parents whom they consider overprotective, underprotective, and reasonably protective. In most neighborhoods, parents quickly get a sense for who "smothers" children and who "lets them run loose." We see which parents are waiting at the bus stops with their teenagers; we see which four-year-olds are riding two-wheelers down the road.

Where do you fit in? How do your policies and the constraints you impose compare to the ones set by other parents? Who seems extreme, rigid, or excessive?

Summing Up So Far

These general guidelines are applicable to most protective decisions we will be facing. Each stage of a child's development, however, presents very specific considerations, and it is often comforting to know exactly what other parents in your situation are dealing with. You might now wish to turn to the chapter that deals with your child's stage of development, or, if you're a new parent, you might want to scan all the chapters of part 2 to see what lies ahead.

PART
TWO

5

Pregnancy and Babies

A first pregnancy can be a nine-month crash course in the art of worry.

> Will I be able to carry the baby to term?
> Will our baby be born healthy?
> Will we be adequate parents? How will we know what to do?
> Have we picked the "best" doctor? The "best" hospital?

The realization comes crashing down upon us: Our actions and choices have consequences for our baby. Expectant mothers worry about the way they've treated their bodies before conception. During pregnancy, they worry about eating well, exercising, not drinking or smoking, being attentive to danger signs, choosing a doctor or birthing center. The baby isn't even born, and already they're wondering if they've been protective enough. Every physical sensation we can't account for in our tower of pregnancy books makes us wonder if we should be doing something we don't even know about to protect our unborn children. It's going to be difficult separating caution from hysteria. We might as well begin discriminating between protective and overprotective behavior.

Perhaps you know people who have chosen to forego parenthood, fearing they'd fail to protect any children they would have from the painful physical or emotional experiences they once endured. Having survived mutilating accidents as a child, Duncan, the son of Garp, in John Irving's novel *The World According to Garp*, vows he will have no children: " 'I couldn't stand watching them grow up.' . . . What [Duncan] meant was, he couldn't stand watching them *not* grow up."

The stakes of our investment are sky-high, for our children will link us to immortality. As author Stephen Langfur writes, "Our children are vulnerable, so we are vulnerable in them." To protect a child is to protect that part of ourselves which we hope might outlast us. Thinking communally, beyond our individual package of genetic material, we know that to protect a child is to protect the continuance of our culture—its values, myths, wisdom, and memories.

Knowing we will shortly become parents transforms us by awakening our protective muscle and showing us how easily we can lose perspective. Margery, a thirty-two-year-old woman who hopes to adopt a baby in Romania, explains: "I have a reputation as a climber. As a kid, I climbed jungle gyms. As an adult, mountains. Now, ever since I've started investigating adoption, I can't pass children playing on a jungle gym without thinking, My God! It's so high up! The handle bars are so far apart—a child could get hurt so easily. I once saw a world filled with wonderful challenges; now I see obstacles and dangers that could hurt a child."

In any phase of parenting—pregnancy included—once we start protecting, we can lose the distinction between protection and overprotection. This goes for male as well as female expectant parents. Kathleen, who is five months pregnant, believes her husband, Buzz, is losing his sense of measure. Buzz can't shake the thought that something will go wrong. "Buzz asked me to stop working out at the gym for fear that I'll have a miscarriage. Our doctor hasn't advised that. On the contrary, the doctor has told me exercise is good. But Buzz has this idea that the baby will be safer if I limit my movements and stay out of crowds and away from young children with germs. When we cross the street, Buzz shields me as if he were a secret service man preventing an assassination attempt."

We worry about our ability to be providers: How much financial security is enough? Some would-be parents vow their own children will not have the same kind of financial anxieties they knew growing up. Nice idea, but given economic reality and the biological limits of the child-bearing years, most of us who do have children end up forgoing the kind of ample security that might provide a cushion against catastrophes and settle for minimal, get-through-each-day security—otherwise we'd never start families. I think of friends of mine, academics, who both grew up in poor families. First, they waited to have a baby until they had finished writing their dissertations and secured tenure-track jobs. Next, they waited until both revised and published their dissertations. They waited a few more years until tenure review. Ultimately, both became tenured, published professors. They owned a lovely Victorian home and had savings in the bank. Then their marriage broke up. Perhaps the wait was for the best: There's one less child who has had to live through divorce. The couple feels otherwise. Neither feels confident remarriage is in the cards. The woman, in particular, worries that her years for conceiving are running out. Both regret that by waiting they may have missed out on ever becoming parents.

Keeping a Sense of Measure

Any pregnancy is a momentous change of life that can seem, as author Elizabeth Kristol describes, more "overwhelming in the abstract" than it is in reality.

Be sure of this: In pregnancy and in any future phase of parenthood, there is no standard, correct way to draw the line between protection and overprotection. Only the individual parent, after a thorough process of consideration, is qualified to make that call. We will be in a better position to work through the process if we familiarize ourselves with situations that may face us and begin to notice how other parents-to-be and new parents are thinking about protection and are working through protective decisions.

What, Me Protect?

Waiting for first babies to come, we see ourselves in a new light. If we were once protected by our own parents and now are finally capable of protecting ourselves and our spouses, we now begin to imagine ourselves as the future protectors of our children. We

- ○ sift through our own memories of being adequately or inappropriately protected;
- ○ analyze the steadiness or vulnerability of our own sense of well-being;
- ○ reflect upon how we handle fear and anxiety;
- ○ scrutinize other families of whom we approve and disapprove; and
- ○ listen to the feedback others give us and decide what to consider and what to ignore.

Ultimately, we are deciding what kind of parent-protectors we wish to become. What kinds of strategies will we choose to navigate dangers with wisdom and measure? What kind of parent-protectors do we seem bound, by genetics and personal history, to become, unless we make an active decision to protect differently?

The Influence of Culture

We need to reflect upon how our cultural origins influence our style of protection. Some of us have inherited a style of protection that continues to be appropriate for our day and age. Others of us, perhaps living in an environment that may be very unlike that of our ancestors, have inherited protective styles that are less suitable.

Betsy, mother of two small daughters, explains her fortunate situation: "My ancestors were settlers, American pioneers. My family has the memory of encountering and mastering physical challenges, reaching rivers and forging them. So I came equipped with a heritage of confidence. When faced with misfortune, we know what to do and we go on. It has passed on to me, and I hope to pass that confidence on to my children. My husband, John, is Armenian. There's pain and violence in his cultural memory, so he's come to parenthood equipped with a heritage of vulnerability. As a person and as a parent, he is fearful. 'If good fortune is mine or my children's at the moment,' says John, 'I cling to it desperately, do everything I can to make it last and let no one take it away from me.'"

Betsy has inherited a model of protection that gives her self-confidence, and she wants to transmit that legacy to her children. John's cultural heritage predisposes him to fear and keeps him constantly awake to vulnerability; as much as he might want to shake off the pessimistic attitude and hypervigilant stance he has inherited, it's not so easy. It becomes even more difficult for John, whose living relatives, noticing his attempts to sidestep his cultural orientation, criticize him and make him feel as if he were putting his children at risk by letting them go outside in cold weather or play rugged sports. John's parents complain: "You're forgetting who you are." John has no intention of forgetting the tragedies Armenians have known, and no intention of failing to steep his children in their Armenian heritage and memory. He is very eager to teach his children to understand why history has made his people fearful, and he hopes his children will become adults who value peace and fight for it.

A Protective Ethic

If we've experienced political and social difficulties in our own lives, we may feel strongly that we have to prepare our children for any similar difficulties we expect they'll encounter. We may begin to articulate a protective ethic for our children as soon as they come into our lives.

John, a South African who has come to MIT to study engineering, is the father of a seventeen-month-old. John explains: "For my child, I am more concerned about victimization than about anything else. I will try to teach him what his rights are in any given situation. I will teach him to fight for his rights, if he must. That's what independence is all about: knowing what your rights are, standing up for them, knowing when you need to run away.

"I'm concerned that my son have a clear sense of fairness. I grew up living with many restrictions: you can't live in that neighborhood; you can't go to that school. I'm concerned that because my son is black, he will grow up with a feeling of being inhibited wherever we live. That is more important to me than anything else: I want to protect him from feeling inhibited because of his color. If I educate him to know his rights and responsibilities and help him to have a good self-image, this will be a better form of protection than my always hovering over him and saying 'Do this, don't do that.' That kind of protection, I believe, is dangerous."

John's concerns for his son, based on his own experiences of discrimination, seem realistic enough. We'd want to be on the lookout if the protective ethic we were articulating was out of touch with the real dangers our children could reasonably expect to face.

Given My Background, How Could I Possibly Be an Adequate Protector?

Those of us who feel we were inadequately protected may go overboard as we attempt to fashion ourselves into better protectors for our children. Jodie has just become pregnant, and along with the anticipation and excitement she feels comes real terror. "Growing up, we were never protected: we were hungry, we went to school with our hair uncombed, our clothes unwashed. Now I observe how my sister Caren, who is eight months pregnant, and I are preparing ourselves in different ways to become adequate protectors.

"Caren prepares to keep her baby from harm by thinking in advance about every contingency. She can name every complication of pregnancy, every emergency of labor and delivery. Far in advance of her delivery date, she's childproofed her whole house. Nothing breakable is lower than four feet off the ground, and every electric socket is plugged up."

Jodie thinks this is overprotection. "My sister's smothering her baby with precautionary measures long before they're needed." She, on the other hand, is trying to get a fix on the role worry should play in parenthood. "I think there are two kinds of worry," Jodie decided. "There's *needless worry*, which I want to avoid—thoughts like, 'What if my husband and I both lost our jobs and couldn't feed our child?' or 'What if our baby was born with some terrible, incurable disease?' Then there's *concerned worry*, which I guess is okay, maybe even a good thing. It's when you focus all your energy and concerns into thoughts, prayers, or necessary actions for the child you're worried about."

Jodie has wisely been searching for role models among the parents she knows. One parent who's made her peace with the limits of protection particularly impresses her. "My friend was always overprotective of her hyperactive six-year-old son, spending so much psychic energy trying to protect him, to little avail. His school psychologist advised her to accept that her child's nature was to hurl himself at the world. Now that she's accepted her son is going to get hurt instead of always trying to stand guard against it, she's much calmer."

Of course, just because we can recognize moderate protection in other parents doesn't always mean we can recognize our own immoderation. Jodie has been reading up on family relations, hoping this will help her heal the hurt she carries from her family of origin. "I'm committed to be in and out of counseling my whole life, because I fear things from my past will pop up that will harm my baby. I can't even anticipate what those 'things' will be. I just live in fear that the way my own parents saw the world will surface in me one day when my guard is down, and I won't even know I've become dysfunctional like my own parents."

I tell Jodie she reminds me of her sister who's childproofing her house for an infant who won't be moving out of its cradle for months. What if the psychic crises she anticipates never happen?

Jodie gets the analogy but still remains on guard. "Panic, fear, and rage are buried deeply inside me. What if my child taps into that deep, shadowy essence of who I am?" she asks.

Being vigilant and anticipating the future is obviously a fine trait for a parent. In parenting, as in other areas of our lives, we prepare for any number of things, anticipating the worst even though it may never happen. We carry umbrellas, buy snow tires, note the emergency exits on planes, save for rainy days, purchase all forms of insurance. Once we've taken steps to protect ourselves, we can relax a little, letting the worst possible outcomes recede in our thoughts. Such forms of precaution are socially encouraged; for example, if we didn't have insurance, we'd be considered irresponsible.

Is Jodie being protective or overprotective in her vow to seek continual counseling? Only Jodie can judge if she's going overboard, anticipating and preparing for problems that might seem too unlikely from anyone else's point of view. Hopefully Jodie will keep her eye on her moderate mentors and remain alert to how easily protective behavior can become overprotective.

The Impact of Prenatal Testing

Unfortunately, advances in medical science have intensified, not lessened our worries during pregnancy. I realized this one day when I heard what I told my daughter, who asked, "What do you call that thing you have before a baby is born?"

"Amniocentesis? Chorionic villus sampling?" I offered. "A sonogram? Alphafetoprotein screening?" I trembled speaking these words, recalling those horrible days of waiting for my doctor to telephone with prenatal test results.

My daughter looked at me as if I has truly lost it. "No— I was thinking about a baby shower."

Once a pregnancy is confirmed, most OB/GYNs advise we test for genetic diseases and maladies that might effect our fetuses. At one time, expectant parents prepared emotionally for the possibility of a less-than-perfect or seriously afflicted baby. Now we feel we may have to take action to spare a child a short life or a life that will be afflicted with disease or physical imperfection. My intention here isn't to evaluate the relative safety of these tests or to debate the moral issue of whether we should have the option of aborting the imperfect or seriously disabled fetus. My concern is to indicate how seriously these tests our doctors are offering—or are imposing upon us—can unhinge us, causing us to lose perspective on protection.

Many of us who will agree to, or who have already experienced, such tests, which are supposed to offer us peace of mind, end up experiencing the testing process as a hellish ordeal, particularly when "abnormalities" often turn out, after further testing, to be "false positives." One week we're mourning the baby in our womb who will be seriously defective, the next week—after a retest—never mind, we learn the baby is perfectly normal. In a provocative article, "Picture Perfect: The Politics of Prenatal Testing," Elizabeth Kristol explains that in prenatal tests such as CVS and amniocentesis, "an initial tap may prove unsuccessful. The doctor may fail to draw enough fluid, he may obtain urine instead of amniotic fluid, or cells in the sample may fail to grow. In such instances, the procedure may have to be repeated, which compounds risk to the patient." In AFP testing, which can be inaccurate, doctors detecting high levels of AFP will repeat the test. According to protocol of the American College of Obstetricians and Gynecologists, "If the second test also comes back positive they are to do an ultrasound. . . . If that is inconclusive, they are to advance to amniocentesis. If that is abnormal, they are to perform a high-resolution ultrasound. With each subsequent test, there is an increased chance that any number of anomalies, slight or severe, may be detected."

Given the inaccuracies of prenatal testing and the risk of miscarriage and birth defects it may pose, Kristol asks the difficult question that most expectant parents under medical care must also ask: "How is it that perfectly healthy women may find themselves having a series of medical tests, some of which pose distinct risks to themselves or their children? The typical pregnant woman would be disturbed to realize that a good deal of the testing that goes on is motivated by factors that are, at best, tangentially related to her well-being or the health of her child." Kristol believes that the public-health sector has motivations for these tests—such as reducing health-care costs to society—which are not the same as a parent's motivations.

For expectant parents, testing that appears to be helpful and informative can invite a state of truly untenable anxiety, particularly when the screening technology obliges them to make godlike decisions. As Kristol puts it, "Certainly, worrying is a natural part of any pregnancy: Can my body do all the things necessary to carry the baby to term? Will the baby be healthy? Will I be a good parent? . . . But in the past few decades, the normal anxieties of pregnancy have been inflamed by a highly specific set of specters—specters prompted less by genuine health threats than by the promotion of certain tests."

Babies

Our babies depend upon us completely for protection. We're intimately, physically connected to them—feeding them in our arms, rocking them for hours, toting or slinging them on our chests or backs. "I thought you already had the baby!" people tease when they see the Snugli bulging out from under a parent's coat. Our babies do seem to be appendages to our bodies. In the earliest months, we so identify with our babies' needs that the point where we stop and our babies begin is blurred.

We're not the only mammals who intensely protect newborns: A mother panda will stay with her infant for as long as twenty-five days, not leaving to feed or defecate, consuming the infant's wastes to keep away predators. (Unlike humans, after two and a half years or so the panda will chase her baby off, so she can mate again!)

It feels almost impossible to overprotect babies. After all, they cannot fend for themselves, they cannot attend to their own needs, and they cannot anticipate harm.

Crossing the Line: When the Terror Doesn't Stop

If so much protection is appropriate for babies, how can we tell when we've crossed the line and have become overprotective?

In *Baby Doctor*, pediatrician and writer Perri Klass describes her first night on call as an intern in a neonatal intensive care unit. She is in charge of minuscule babies, many whose lives hang by a thread. That first night, Dr. Klass is tense, hungry, deprived of sleep, and "souped up on adrenaline." Klass assures herself that the terror she feels is appropriate: "I've just made an enormous leap," she says, from medical student to real doctor; her responsibility is huge, her skills new and untested.

What if you, too, feel terrorized the first night, the first weeks, the first month that you're home taking care of your healthy, newborn baby? *You probably will be!* You, like Dr. Klass, have good reason for your terror. Sleepless, dreamless, and perhaps clueless about the ins and outs of baby care, you're convinced your success in meeting your newborn's needs comes as something of a miracle. Having this baby has aroused passionate love and an overwhelming concern. The very intensity of these unfamiliar feelings leaves you weak-kneed and stumbling.

Consider the thoughts that cause new parents to toss in bed as their infant sleeps.

> Will we be able to hear our baby cry at night?
> What if we don't know how to respond to his needs?
> Is he too warm? Too cold?
> If he's being breast-fed, is he really getting enough to eat? If he's being bottle-fed, is he missing out on critical antibodies?
> Is that just a cough or is it pneumonia?
> How can we be sure he isn't one of those babies who gets smothered in the night or dies of SIDS?
> What if other babies seem to be doing more or to be growing faster than our baby?
> What if something we do now—spoiling him or not paying enough attention—will effect him for the rest of his life?
> Is all our baby equipment safe, or are we going to hear that something has been recalled by the manufacturer?
> If we take the baby to the park in his carriage and turn away for a minute, will he be kidnapped?

Developing Confidence

Feeling overwhelmed by your baby some or even much of the time doesn't necessarily mean you're overprotecting. Ed, father of a fourteen-week-old baby, claims he often feels overwhelmed and out of control. "When my baby cries and I don't know what he's crying about, I think, Something is seriously wrong here. Should we call the doctor? Being responsible for this tiny person who can't tell me what's the matter frightens me. I have to read all these subtle signs, and I think, What if I'm totally wrong? When I hear of a baby with a terrible problem, I imagine, What if my baby has that problem, and I don't even know? I refer to the child-care books and feel somewhat relieved when I get the information I need."

As the days pass, it is Ed's flourishing baby who assures him he can handle the daily tasks and crises of parenthood. "Now the baby is almost four months old, and I have to admit, I'm getting used to him, especially since he's survived his first cold. You can almost say I'm confident. If there's something really wrong, the baby will let us know eventually."

Developing Skills

If our own parents were competent and self-assured as parents, we may be a step ahead of the game, even with our first babies. "Because of my upbringing, I felt well-prepared to be a parent," says Leni. "I was the oldest of six. My mother was happy to be a full-time homemaker, and she focused her whole being on us and our home. She always had a remedy for any sickness or injury."

From the time Leni became a parent, she felt confident. "It wasn't just my mother I could turn to; there was an extended family of wise, competent relatives. Growing up, I was used to seeing people cope in various ways when things happened that were beyond our control."

Leni acknowledges that despite her background, taking care

of her first baby did initially arouse some anxiety. "Though I had seen my parents successfully handle the very same situations, knowing how to do something in your head is different that actually doing it. I knew what my mother did for a feverish baby, but I had never done it myself. By the time I had my second child and had weathered many fevers, I was truly confident."

Much of the anxiety new parents feel—anxiety that can translate into overprotection—comes from their not knowing what to do in response to a baby's day-to-day behavior, not knowing what's normal and what's not, and not knowing where to turn for help. Feeling inept, helpless, or alone, we can convince ourselves that we will damage our fragile baby. At times, we may even wish the baby was back in the womb again, safe from our awkward ministrations!

What Comes—and Goes— with the Territory

Brand-new parents just home from the hospital may feel that if they don't keep guard, their babies will stop breathing. New parents may wake their pediatricians in the middle of the night when their babies have a spell of coughing or run a temperature. This kind of overprotection comes with the territory—and generally *goes* with it. As Jill, mother of a three-month-old explains, "When I first held Maya, she would scream frantically, even though she was fed, dry, and rested. I worried about what could happen. What if she held her breath and passed out? Finally, I learned that this screaming is just what Maya does when she is frustrated. The screaming—which stops if I massage her back—won't hurt her. I was also worried Maya wasn't developing as fast as the baby across the street, who rolled over long before she did. At first, I tried to play games with her, to encourage her to roll. Now I figure, she'll learn at her own pace."

Getting Help

Say your baby is six months old by now and you're still worrying that you won't meet her needs or detect some terrible illness unless you keep a constant vigil. Say you are still so frightened of germs that you refuse to let anyone near your baby and you shudder at the thought of taking her in public. Say every protective situation you consider is the red light that tells you to hold on tightly.

You might look out for ways to build your confidence, and in doing so, you might be able to identify more of the green-light situations that will allow you to let go. Tried and true methods, such as joining hospital or community-run parenting classes, joining parents' groups, or seeking out a pediatric nurse practitioner who encourages you to ask all the questions you think are too stupid, are all ways to begin replacing the terror that comes with ignorance with the calm that comes with having facts and reassurance. "Once I started taking the parenting class," Jill said, "I stopped worrying so much and relaxed. I learned how to play with the baby, learned how to anticipate what's coming up. We learned baby CPR, met with a pediatric dentist, a family therapist, learned infant massage. I could ask the instructor anything. Now that the class is over, we parents keep meeting once a week to share what's going on. It's not so much answers I need anymore, but the reassurance that other babies are going through the same phases as Maya." If you ask veteran parents for help, they won't think you're hopeless. Chances are, they'll be happy to encourage you and pass on the same advice and simple solutions they once gratefully received.

If you can anticipate experiencing high anxiety in advance, if you and your spouse are truly clueless about baby care, if neither friends nor family members are available for help and reassurance, consider engaging a postpartum doula. Neither a baby nurse nor a housekeeper, a doula comes to your home and offers whatever assistance, care, and education the new parent needs.

In time, as you acquire your parenting "sea legs," you will develop a sense of knowing when something is really wrong. You will know how to calm a distressed baby. You will know what's a little sniffle, what's a call-the-pediatrician-in-the-morning sickness, and what demands a dash to the emergency room. You will be better prepared to let your baby experience more of the world outside the nursery; and when friends offer to hold your baby for a while, you'll jump at the chance for some respite, without any of the fears you once had about germs. You will learn to read your own child and react appropriately to the cues she gives you. Instead of rigidly doing things for your baby, you will synchronize your care with her needs and moods. You will also learn what veteran parents know: When you've protected your baby adequately and have eliminated the possibility of risk, you are allowed to take a breath.

Second Time Around

If you feel you overprotected your first baby, you may be happily surprised to find out that by the time number two comes along, many of your overprotective tendencies have gone out the window. You are more confident, more realistic, and, frankly, too exhausted to fret when it's unnecessary. Veteran parents joke that children who come after the first one flourish because they don't have our undivided attention or the complete bounty of our fussiness.

Mothers/Fathers

Many a new mother, despite her commitment to feminism, egalitarianism, and shared parenting, surprises herself when she discovers that she has strong doubts that her husband can protect the baby as well as she can. Many a new father, anticipating he'll play a major role in baby care, finds himself either shut out or retreating because he's been made to feel so inept and lacking in proper instincts.

Kathleen, mother of two-month-old Huck, tells a common tale: "At first, I worried when it was Tim's turn to take care of Huck. Tim seemed so uncertain about what clothes to put on, how to snap the onesies, or even how to attach the diaper. I had to tell Tim what the different cries meant. He was ready to let Huck cry it out, as that's how he was raised, but the books I've read say 'Go to your baby right away,' as responding to a baby builds self-esteem. I insisted Tim respond, but I never knew if that's what he did. Once, when I had a friend's wedding shower to go to, I almost brought the baby along because I was afraid to leave him with Tim. In the end, I did go alone, because I knew I needed to show Tim I had confidence in him—the same way he's shown that he has had confidence in me right from the start. Of course, I really had no confidence—but I still went. I must have called home three times, and they were doing just fine."

Because few of us were raised by mothers and fathers who shared the tasks of child care, we find ourselves in the position of having to invent the wheel if we want to move away from the model of "mother protects, father provides." We may be carrying one or all of the following outmoded beliefs:

Women innately know what to do with babies.

Women are especially attuned to babies.

Women know about child care from having played with dolls.

Women are gentler and naturally more selfless than men, and men won't put babies' needs before their own.

Men will button babies' clothes backwards, feed them the wrong foods, and toss them up in the air and injure them.

If we let these beliefs influence us, we jeopardize our efforts to establish families in which mothers and fathers can protect and provide. As Kathleen discovered, mothers and fathers need to boost each other's confidence, not diminish it. Mothers and fathers need to trust that different styles of care giving and different styles of playing won't harm a baby. In fact, the differences foster adaptability.

What if one parent (usually the mother) carries the bulk of baby care and the second parent is on the scene for only part of the time? Jill, whose life fits this common pattern, explains, "I always keep my husband up to date about what Maya can do and what her sleeping and eating patterns are, because they keep changing. That way, Todd can always take over without much explanation. I know he'll play with Maya differently than I would, but I figure, that's lucky for her."

Handling Big Problems

Having information at hand and a plan to deal with problems that arise save us from being swamped by the fears that would lead us to overprotect. If you have suspected that your baby has a problem, usually discovering precisely what is wrong and beginning to formulate a treatment plan will put you back into the range of adequate protecting. Knowledge, even if it's bad news, tempers fear and gives us the power to cope. As Dr. Joseph LeDoux, a leading researcher in brain mapping at New York University, explains, "Feeling deeply anxious is often a result of feeling fearful about something without understanding why or what you are fearful of." When Sheldon finally learned his one-year-old son Jason was unresponsive because he had a hearing disorder, his nightmares about Jason falling from cliffs and slipping into rushing rivers stopped. "With the difficult news in my hands, there was no need for me to imagine other nightmarish scenarios."

Thinking Toward the Future

Parents of babies find themselves discussing—or heatedly arguing about—just how much protection is appropriate. The green or red lights that are simple for one parent may be challenging or difficult for the other. Your baby's infancy is a good time to begin articulating attitudes for ourselves and for each other, to get a sense of where we see eye to eye and where we don't. "We're always discussing protection," says Jeff, father of two-month-old Tori. "There's a wide gulf between what each of us considers protection and overprotection. I tend to think I'll want to step back and let Tori decide his own path. It's not that I don't plan to be concerned for him always, it's just that I want to allow him to be responsible for making his own decisions. I'm more relaxed than my wife. She worries about Tori being corrupted by violence on television, having his intelligence stunted. When our TV died and Carmen felt we shouldn't replace it for Tori's sake, I said, 'Forget it.' That's going overboard. We weren't protected from TV growing up, and we turned out okay."

Carmen doesn't feel Jeff is representing her point of view accurately: "I don't think either of us will be overprotective or authoritative. Being authoritative won't make me be more secure. I'll feel more secure about Tori if we can teach him how to be a good decision maker, if he can affirm good values. You can't tell kids what to do, but you can teach them what's right and just."

Advantages of Not Seeing Eye to Eye

In my own marriage, I've always felt our different attitudes toward protection have been, for our children, a blessing and have helped us notice when one of us is overprotecting. My husband Peter has a greater sense of physical abandon; on snowy days, he'll take the children sledding from the highest point on the hillside. (I would have us stay indoors by the fire and read.) Knowing I might contaminate the fun and freedom with my terror, I will often choose not to participate in such expeditions and do not share my misgivings with the children.

On the other hand, Peter has seen devastating illness in his own family, which might account for the fact that when the girls sneeze or run a fever, he imagines the worst disease possible. When I've been away for a few days and Peter has been the only parent in charge, I'm not surprised if he's taken someone either to the pediatrician for a throat culture or to the emergency room for an X ray of what turns out to be growing pains. As it happens, I am calmer when it comes to physical symptoms, perhaps because I'm still bending over backwards not to be as hysterical and pessimistic about health as my own mother. When Peter and I are both around, and the girls complain of aches or pains, my tempering influence allows us to wait a day or so in case symptoms subside—and they usually do. If Peter still insists that a child needs medical treatment and I still think he's making something out of nothing, then he'll make the appointment and take the child to the doctor.

I must not mislead you: When we became parents we did not automatically negotiate the effective give-and-take of our different protective styles. We've been parents for fifteen years now, and over those years we've flung many an epithet at each other. And after fifteen years of give-and-take and of surviving a number of trying situations, we've come to a consensus and have arrived at what amounts to a policy. We've decided to consider that the less protective parent in any situation isn't being cavalier, just less burdened with the baggage of anxiety. Therefore, the parent who takes the lead is the parent who is temporarily calmer, more confident, and less apt to restrict or take a drastic measure.

Even Babies Need to Move Toward
Greater Independence

Some of the wisest insights into the ways parents adapt, first to their baby's total dependence and then to their baby's gradual move toward independence and separateness (sometimes referred to as "individuation"), come from the work of British child psychiatrist D. W. Winnicott. You may be familiar with Winnicott's term the "good enough mother"; he defines the caregiver as one

> *who makes active adaptation to the infant's needs, and active adaptation that gradually lessens, according to the infant's growing ability to account for failure or adaptation and to tolerate the results of frustration. Naturally, the infant's own mother is more likely to be good enough than some other person, since this active adaptation demands an easy and unresented preoccupation with one infant; in fact, success in infant care depends on the fact of devotion, not on cleverness or intellectual enlightenment.*

If devotion to one's baby is a good thing, are there boundaries to devotion to look out for? Can a parent be too devoted to a baby? I think not. Our devotion represents our commitment to love our baby and to put the baby's needs above our own, no matter what they are, regardless of our own circumstances. We do need, however, to notice when we are failing to identify the times when our babies must start to meet their own needs and begin to fend for themselves, even in the tiniest ways, as they mature. Winnicott calls this a "gradual failing of adaptation," on the part of the caregiver, which follows the "high degree of adaptation" the newborn requires.

For instance, if we dash to pick up our babies every time we hear them peep, this is not devotion but a form of overprotection. By dashing over, we prohibit a baby from experiencing those minute moments of productive frustration that will lead to new accomplishments. In baby terms, we need to let go some. This might mean waiting for the baby to turn over to get a better glimpse of a mobile or waiting for the baby to find a thumb and suck it for comfort instead of providing a pacifier, encouraging the baby to fall back to sleep without having to be held and rocked each time. These are some of the letting-go activities that gradually allow a baby to experience being separate from his or her caregiver and to develop what we call a "self." Some parents refuse to recognize the points at which their babies are able to entertain themselves or to offer signals indicating they are wet, hungry, sleepy, or bored. In their overattentiveness, in their overeagerness to anticipate and attend to their babies' needs, parents prohibit their babies from advancing and achieving competence as they naturally would. This can cause real trouble. Deborah Jacobvitz and her colleagues at the University of Texas at Austin have noted that "intrusive caregiving patterns during the first year of life increase children's vulnerability to later social and emotional patterns. Six-month-old infants whose caregivers engaged in intrusive and interfering behaviors . . . have been shown to develop anxious attachments with their mothers at 12 and 18 months."

Attitude: A Lust for Life

Right from the start we communicate our attitude toward life to our children. If we have a lust for living, if we want to suck the very marrow out of life, we communicate that. If life and the unknown terrify us, and we find comfort only in seclusion and regularity, we communicate that. Colby, a thirty-seven-year-old mother living in Seattle, communicates her exuberance, which in turn is reflected in her robust, high-spirited little daughter, a child whom I've heard others describe as being "full of beans." "I really love life," says Colby. "It's the greatest thing you can know and I want my daughter to have it. When she was a little baby, I didn't want to keep her indoors. I had an easy birth—a healthy baby just came out—and right away I wanted to take her out to the park to smell real air, not the overprocessed, overheated, mist-machined air so many babies get. I went for a walk in the snow with my five-day-old baby. 'Livia,' I said to her, 'this is snow!' I would watch other parents whom I thought were overprotective, with their perfect strollers, piles of blankets, coordinated buntings, designer hats—it drove me nuts! All this zealousness. I thought, Their protection is bullshit! My baby wants symmetry of life, she wants the warmth of my body. I wanted her next to me and held her in a carrier. For me, that was protective. I fed her immediately, I carried her for months—that was protective; that's what I knew she needed. When she was ready to eat solid foods, I never fed her with a spoon. After slowly introducing foods to test for allergies, I'd eventually blend together carrots with dill, sautéed mushrooms, steak. I'd serve three little puddles on her tray, and I'd let Livia find the food, smear it, put it in her mouth as best she could. She discovered: This is food! It tastes good. Today, at five, she has a gorgeous, lean body; she eats everything. Her only problem is dealing with other children who tease her for scarfing down bacon and avocados. When she was ready to 'cruise' on her own, she had capable, rubbery legs, for I hadn't been telling her, as other parents do, 'You'll fall! You'll fall!' I knew she was ready to leave my body. I wanted my child to discover life on her own terms."

Making Protective Decisions

Jane Martin of Titusville, New Jersey, is the founder of the Natural Baby Catalog, which offers "alternative"—that is, nontoxic and environmentally safe—products for children, and she is the mother of a baby and two young children. Considering Jane's many concerns about toxicity and pollution, I suspected she might be totally angst-ridden and hypervigilant—in a word, overprotective. She's not. She has discovered a multitude of alternative products and creative solutions to alleviate her concerns. Acknowledging she can't make the world a more protected place for children overnight, she regularly makes compromises.

Her middle-of-the road policy: "If the product or piece of equipment is just too essential to your life, you have to use it. If you can find a safe alternative you can trust that isn't much different, use it."

One night shortly before I spoke to her, Jane had made a compromise. She and the children were sleeping over at her mom's, and the man her mother lives with, like a grandfather to the children, was making waffles for them from a mix. Jane scanned the ingredients on the package and saw artificial coloring listed. She had to decide if she should prohibit her children from eating the waffles that were lovingly being made for them. Jane let them have the waffles. First of all, she figured, they're not eating them every day. Second, Jane recognized her children's emotional well-being needed protection as much as their physical well-being. She didn't want them to feel terrified of poisons all around them, especially if they could be offered by people who professed to love and care for them.

Jane advises first-time parents who want to protect children in a potentially toxic world to read widely with an open mind and to think for themselves. Don't, Jane advises, let doctors make the decisions for you: "Doctors are inclined to do something for a sick child, even if there's really nothing much to be done. When you go to a doctor and beg, 'Please do something for my child,' it's hard for the doctor to take your fifty dollars and say, 'There's nothing I can do for you.'"

If you find yourself, like Jane, making protective decisions that aren't mainstream (such as choosing not to inoculate, not to use antibiotics, or not to use disposable diapers), you will need to arm yourself with knowledge and find ways to boost your confidence in your alternative solutions to conventional child-rearing practices.

Some Signs that You May Be Overprotecting the Child You're Expecting or Your New Baby

You

❑ worry that every complication of pregnancy and childbirth will happen to you;

❑ worry that every disorder fetuses and newborns might experience will happen to your child;

❑ go overboard on restricting your movements during pregnancy, even when your doctor has not advised this;

❑ keep vigil by your new baby for fear something will happen;

❑ continually call the doctor with "emergencies";

❑ fear that everyone will contaminate your child with germs;

❑ are convinced your baby isn't getting enough nutrition, even when his growth indicates he's doing fine;

❑ are convinced something is wrong with your baby's development, even when you're reassured it's normal;

❑ refuse to trust that your spouse or partner can take care of the baby as well as you can.

Things You Can Do to Let Go

Before the Baby Comes

❑ Enroll in a childbirth preparation class.

❑ Enroll in a parenting skills class for expectant parents.

❑ Spend time observing how parents you admire negotiate the daily tasks of child rearing and resolve their concerns.

❑ Find an obstetrician or nurse-midwife who attends to your concerns and reassures you.

After the Baby Comes

❏ Determine if the pediatrician or nurse-practitioner you have engaged really listens to your concerns and offers the help and reassurance you need. If the "chemistry" isn't right, search out another practice.

❏ Join a parents group. Often the alumni of childbirth preparation classes remain together for support and companionship.

❏ Get help at home.

❏ Leave your baby in good hands for a short time, at least so you can take a breather and regain some perspective.

❏ Recognize that you are setting up a long-term problem for yourself and your child if you insist that no one—not even your partner—can care for the baby in your absence.

❏ Read widely and trust that you will be able to select the child-care advice that's best for you and your child.

❏ Get specific guidelines from your doctor about when it's necessary to call regarding a child's fever, diarrhea, and vomiting.

If You Are About to Become a Parent or Have a Baby, These Are Some of the Protective Decisions You Are Likely to Be Making

Whom will you turn to for prenatal care? An OB/GYN? A birthing center? A nurse-midwife?

Will you take all the prenatal testing recommended to you?

If you are adopting, which route is most likely to be speedy and least likely to result in heartbreak?

What kinds of paints, wallpaper, and flooring will you use to prepare the baby's room?

What kinds of cribs, bumpers, baby carriers, and car seats are the safest?

Are the pieces of baby equipment you've received as hand-me-downs in keeping with the most recent safety guidelines? Will your baby sleep in your room, and if so, for how long? Are the toys your baby plays with large enough not to be ingested?

Who is the best medical caregiver for your child? A family doctor? A pediatrician? A nurse practitioner? A holistic, natureopathic, or homeopathic doctor?

With whom is the baby safe? You? Your spouse? A relative? A baby-sitter?

Will taking your baby outside expose him or her to germs or to too much sun or cold?

Will you breast-feed or bottle-feed? How do you determine if your baby is getting enough to eat? How will you tell if your baby is developing appropriately?

When do you call the doctor? How do you know if you're making a mountain out of a molehill?

Whose advice or criticism do you take seriously? Whose do you ignore? When do you search for a second opinion?

Once you begin to acquire more knowledge about raising your baby, when can you trust your own judgment, no matter what anyone else says?

6

Toddlers and Preschoolers

At no time do we experience letting go of our children in a more visceral way than when they are toddlers and pre-schoolers. They yearn—on occasion—to break away from the safety of our arms. We, in turn, must allow and encourage them to explore the capacity of their bodies, adventure within the contours of their environment, and encounter the people of their small world who might love and intrigue them. In all these excursions outward, we must permit them to take little falls.

Separation Anxiety: Whose Anxiety Is It?

If we're anxious about being apart from our small children, we're tempted to overprotect. I think of Jesse, whose mother brought him to a morning nursery school at the beginning of the year. Jesse's mother, Mia, planned only to stay for the first morning or two of school, as many of the mothers or fathers did. She stayed for two months.

Until then, three-year-old Jesse had never been left with a baby-sitter or his grandparents. "I didn't believe he'd be okay without me," Mia explains. "I felt I was the only one who could take care of him. I was intensely possessive."

The first and second mornings of school went by, and every parent but Mia had gone. Mia sat on the floor on the edge of the classroom; she hovered on the periphery of the playground when the children went outdoors.

"How could I leave?" Mia asked. "The children had to line up to wash in the bathroom and Jesse couldn't negotiate all the moves they made. Even getting up on the little stool at the sink frustrated him. Every time there was a transition to a new activity or a new place, he had a hard time. I needed to be there to comfort him when it got tough." Jesse's difficulties come as no surprise: Preschoolers whose caregivers have been intrusive are typically easily frustrated by problem-solving tasks.

Mia could see that other children were learning to swallow their feelings about separation, yet when she began to make little overtures to leave, Jesse kicked and screamed. At this stage of the game, Mia was stumped. This was a yellow light for her. Should she stick around, or should she go? She didn't know.

In retrospect, Mia realized that the longer she stayed, the worse she made it for Jesse. "He was constantly anxious, because he never knew when I would leave. If I had said goodbye early on, then he and I would have dealt with the separation as the other families had; this way, the whole process was prolonged. But I couldn't leave. How can a parent walk out on a crying child?"

Near the end of the second month, Mia overheard the teachers whisper, "The kid is fine, but what's the matter with the mother?" They were finally assertive with Mia, saying to her, "Jesse is going to be all right here by himself." With those signals from the teachers, Mia understood that while she might never be ready to leave, Jesse had long been ready to have her go. She recognized his resourcefulness: He could go to the bathroom alone, clean off the snack table, move toward a nice child and away from an aggressive one. He would be okay. Finally, a green light.

The next year, Mia signed Jesse up for a gymnastics class

and found separating difficult once again. "Jesse wouldn't let me out of the room. The teacher wanted the children to be physically free, but Jesse isn't a risk-taking child. He is quiet, very cautious, aware of how easy it is to get hurt." For Mia, this was a red light, and she took Jesse out of the class.

Was this the best decision? Was it really Jesse who wouldn't let his mother out of the room, or, once again, was it Mia who couldn't bear to leave? Why does separation present so much challenge at each juncture—more so for Mia, it seemed to me, than for her son? When I speak to Mia when Jesse is five, she acknowledges she is always dealing with her own sense of being abandoned by her brother, who died years ago in a hiking accident. Her feeling of abandonment is reactivated each time Jesse is on the cusp of leaving her. When she watches Jesse grow more self-sufficient emotionally and physically, she feels as if she is losing him and their intimate relationship. The fact is Mia knows she ought to be fostering Jesse's independence; she knows her protectiveness must change as Jesse keeps developing—but the right time to let go never seems to come. It was so much easier when Jesse was a tiny baby, when she was never pressed to let Jesse go.

Mia is convinced that her inability to separate is connected to having lost her brother, after whom Jesse is named. "It's an intense loss," says Mia, "and I have never recovered from it." As Mia deeply overidentifies with her son at each juncture of separation, she reexperiences many of her own past losses, especially that of her brother. Researchers at the University of Texas at Austin explain situations such as Mia's: When their children are distressed, caregivers who are preoccupied with their own unmet needs experience their children's distress as their own.

Protecting Our Children . . .
and Not Ourselves

Our small children can help us notice when our own pasts influence us to protect in an unrealistic manner. Catherine, mother of five-year-old Ada, explains: "I grew up with rigid, authoritative parents who imposed tight boundaries on me: There was no room for diverse thinking, asking questions, venturing to unknown places, acting on your curiosity. Having been raised in such a home, I fear rigidity and worry welling up in me, and they do. But I've noticed that Ada can joke about my worries. I trust that her native resistance, which I wouldn't dare stifle, will keep me from overprotecting her. She'll say, 'Oh, Mama, you're doing it again' or 'You're the best-worst mother I've ever had!' Unlike my parents, I encourage Ada to challenge me, even though I'm still clearly in charge as the parent. When she says, 'Mama, you need a time out!' she's not being cheeky—she's right!" Paying attention to Ada's reactions has helped Catherine to be able to say, "Oops—there's the anxious mama!"

Moderating Our Reactions

Letting go doesn't just happen. As our small children grow and no longer require as much hands-on protection, we need to watch for the times when we can begin letting go, either by sitting tight for a spell or by butting out. This is not easy, acknowledges Dr. Roger Granet, clinical associate professor of psychiatry at Cornell Medical College. "It seems instinctual for parents to love, nurture, guide. Maybe it's less instinctual for us to let go—it seems harder for humans than for birds!"

Dr. Shelley Lanzkowsky, a pediatrician and mother of two small children, advises parents that toddlers who fall while they're playing generally don't do well when parents react in a disproportionate manner—gasping, rushing over, coddling the child. "Ideally, I'd like to see the toddler who's fallen on the grass or carpet get up first." In other words, for the moment, sit tight. "I'd wait and see if he cries before I start to get upset." We might need to train ourselves not to assume our toddlers are hurt unless we see some sign of injury or hear them cry or complain. Generally, if we don't overreact to a toddler's everyday tumbles, the toddler gets used to falling down, picking himself up, and going on. When a toddler learns his tumble will produce a splendid reaction on the part of his parents, he comes to anticipate it—and even provoke it.

When it comes to feeding, it's especially hard to overcome our gut reaction, which is to get involved. Children between the ages of two and four often decide out of the blue that they will not eat vegetables, fruit, or meat. It's easy for a parent to worry, to imagine that a child's current eating habits will cause malnutrition and lead to God-knows-what awful consequences. Mealtime becomes tense and nightmarish for everyone. Often, the parent who's more tense, more authoritarian, or more exacting about decorum, will say, "If you don't finish your peas, you can't go outside" or ". . . you can't have your dessert." That parent might suggest that if the other parent gives in to the child on this matter of eating, the child will discover she can "get away with murder" or "have her own way." The feeding battle escalates. Soon it has little to do with the child and everything to do with the parents, who end up arguing over who is really in control of the situation and who really knows what's best for the child.

Intellectually, most of us know it's counterproductive to talk to small children about their food intake or to make threats, promises, or contingencies involving food. We know that it's best to ignore a small child's refusal to eat some particular food; the strike on broccoli usually turns out to be temporary unless it's made into a big deal. In her research, Dr. Lanzkowsky has noted that the more attention the child who fusses about eating gets, the less he will eat. In fact, when the pressure to eat is too intense, children have been known to react by starving themselves. Many of us know this, but still, the urge to protect our child from hunger and malnutrition takes over when we see a plate with carrots and chicken untouched. "The urge to feed is so primitive," says Dr. Lanzkowsky. Despite all of her medical knowledge, Lanzkowsky admits that as a parent "often, I want to tell my son or daughter, 'Just have four more bites.' "

Teaching Safety

The more confident you are that your small child has absorbed your teachings concerning safety, the greater freedom your child can have. Colby, mother of five-year-old Livia, explains: "Livia knows how to distinguish a friend from a stranger, and knows she does not talk to strangers, touch them, or let them touch her. She knows how to be cautious." Still, Colby doesn't let down her protective radar. While Livia is bouncing up and down on a small trampoline at a mutual friend's July Fourth party, I see that Colby has one eye continually on Livia. "I am highly aware that at Livia's age, her willingness to experiment can override all she knows about safety," Colby says. "At her age, her body can easily direct her mind."

With caution, comes freedom. "I can allow Livia to cut her own fruit and vegetables with a sharp knife because I have shown her, over and over again, how quickly a knife cuts and what the consequences can be. She has never yet had an accident with a knife. In general, I try to be forthcoming with her about causes and effects. I don't explore the grotesque or dwell on disgusting details or misery, but I don't buffer the bad news either."

Permitting Individuality

Colby believes she protects Livia by allowing her to become fully herself: "Overall, I try not to edit, to manipulate, to infantilize. My child has a unique spirit which I need to encourage so she can give birth to it. I trust she has a barometer for her own happiness, and I try to read her barometer and ask her questions to figure out where she's at. If she's particularly sullen or distracted, I know it's for a reason. I encourage her to be honest and articulate about what's happening to her. I encourage her to be her own person by allowing her to pick out her own clothes. If she wants to read the same book or play the same game for three weeks, she can."

I, for one, am not so good at cultivating a child's emotional complexity, and I'm not comfortable with emotional explosions. I tell Colby I think of her style of parenting as "cowboy parenting." "You're brave," I tell her.

"Not brave," she says, "I'm respectful. I treat my daughter the way I want to be treated. I must not ignore or dismiss her pain. I must have the courage to witness my child experience all the emotional range." Colby prefers to call her style of parenting "Buddha parenting," and explains: "My child is wise already. Her wisdom comes from knowledge."

Caregivers

In the preschool years, most of us will, at some time or another, be entrusting our children to others. Beyond the issue of separation, which we discussed earlier, we feel real concerns about our ability to judge the quality of care our child will receive. Will the caregiver be loving and cautious or cold and careless? Does the caregiver attend to our child adequately and offer the appropriate kinds of intellectual and motor stimulation? Obviously, we allay some of our concerns about the caregiver's competence when we check out an individual's background and references or look into the reputation of a school or day-care center. If our child is not yet verbal, his or her demeanor at the beginning and end of the day clue us into how things are going, and if our child is speaking, his or her reactions (which we do sometimes have to take with a grain of salt) are also important sources of feedback. But ultimately, it's the assurance we get by watching the caregiver in action and trusting our intuition—our ability to recognize who is loving, who is careful, who is levelheaded, who is fun—that allows us to see a green light and confidently leave our children in someone else's care.

Scott, a physician's assistant and single father with custody of his four-year-old, has already employed three nannies for his son. By now he is confident he can work through the process of engaging a new nanny. He'll take off work for a week and stay home with his son as the new nanny begins work. "I get to know her, gathering information in whatever discrete, nonthreatening ways I can. I fired one nanny after just a day. Forget her glowing references. Having observed her in action, they meant nothing! The rest of the nannies were nice young women, and I just knew it from watching them interact with my son: If she squats down to get to my son's level when she talks to him, you can tell her impulses are good, even if she's not a trained-in-early-education expert. As far as all the nanny-from-hell stories go, I believe you can't defend yourself against all the random lunatics in the universe. The nanny I dismissed turned out to be a pathological liar. She gave me bad vibes immediately. Something was not right: She was too sweet, too obliging, too touchy. Maybe it's because of my medical background, but I feel I can read people by the non-verbal signs they give, despite what they say. If a nanny makes me feel uncomfortable, I trust that gut feeling: I don't feel I have to substantiate it with reason or concrete evidence. I believe I can tell who's a good person, who's responsible. My ex-wife wanted to dismiss a nanny who had wildly teased hair and red painted nails, but after spending time with her, I could just tell that she was really a nice girl. She stayed with us for a year until she went back to school, and my son loved her."

If no caregiver and no environment is good enough for our child, if we never see a green light, we might ask ourselves if we've been realistic in our evaluations. We need to determine what specific evidence we need to find so we can be reassured that our child will flourish in our absence.

Adoption

Adoption poses particular protective issues, and parents who have adopted children from different cultures may feel they shoulder even additional protective burdens. Catherine and Peter are the adoptive parents of four-year-old Ada, who is Korean. Catherine explains: "First of all, we worry about Ada being oriental in a predominantly white culture." Secondly, Catherine and Peter are concerned to provide Ada with enough information about Korea and enough contact with the local Korean community to give her positive feelings about her origins. At the same time, they also worry that if Ada doesn't identify strongly with their own American Baptist culture, she will want to leave them and go back to Korea when she matures. They suppose they will be able to make peace with this eventuality: "If Ada wants to move back to Korea at eighteen, we may have to do that with her, or we'll just visit her often."

Catherine and Peter have observed Ada trying to make her own peace with their bicultural, biracial family, and this reassures them that whatever happens, it will be okay. "Ada likes to pretend she came from my womb," says Catherine. "I once had this big, roomy dress. Ada would crawl under the dress and pretend to be born. At four, she still wants to enact this, so we'll do it with a blanket. It seems like play, but I know that for her it's serious business."

Preschoolers with Special Needs

Parents of small children with special physical, emotional, or social needs quickly discover how easily they can rationalize overprotection by referring to a child's particular set of difficulties, challenges, or misfortunes. Here I offer Kate's story, because it exemplifies how a parent who could so easily justify overprotection chooses, instead, for her son's sake, to protect with measure.

Kate and Terrance have a four-year-old son who has suffered from a rare kidney disease since birth. Jeff, fragile, frail, easily prone to infection, is in and out of hospitals. Despite the scrupulous care Jeff requires, Kate and Terrance strive not to overprotect by hovering and shielding, tempting as that may be. A common cold could land Jeff in intensive care.

"We have to be continually diligent taking his temperature, treating any infection, making sure he gets his medication," says Kate. Jeff's doctors praise Kate for her ability to pick up on a problem. "Sometimes I call the doctor and ask if I'm worried about nothing. I never am; the doctor will tells us to get down to the hospital immediately. So by now, I trust my intuition. If a problem gets out of hand before I can catch it, I feel terrible, but I know that nothing is gained by beating up on myself. I just say, well, I should have done something, but I didn't, and I let it pass."

As a result of Jeff's illness, he is small for his age, and Kate is aware that she must prepare him for and protect him from whatever grief others will give him because of his size. "We call Jeff 'big guy,' and take people aside to nicely explain that just because he's cute and cuddly, he shouldn't be babied. One reason we're holding him back from kindergarten for a year is to give him an extra year for learning social skills and for growth."

Usually, Kate feels confident that her efforts to help Jeff protect himself are working. Getting feedback from others makes her secure: "His preschool teacher says he's a real little scrapper and doesn't take nonsense from anyone. He'll take on the biggest kid if he takes a toy away from him."

I should note here, that when I spoke to Kate, Jeff was going into his third week of running a 103-degree fever that his doctor can't explain. While I would have long lost my cool, Kate is calm. Her "flip-out point," as she calls it, is 105 degrees. "I admit that I can get totally overwhelmed by the responsibility I have as a parent: I feel as if I shoulder a great burden and have no life of my own. I do want out sometimes, I want to escape. It helps if I tell myself, 'There's nothing more that you can do and you're doing everything that you can.' I keep my life as stress-free as possible. I don't watch scary movies or anything about children in abusive families or abduction. I won't even watch the news. I have too much to worry about with Jeff without watching all this."

Some Signs You May Be Overprotecting a Toddler or Preschooler

Your Child

❑ has so many fears of strangers, noises, animals, weather, and traveling that it is a trial every time you leave home;
❑ can't get along with other children without a parent constantly mediating;
❑ is easily frustrated when problems need to be solved;
❑ refuses to use the toilet or is highly anxious about getting to the toilet in time;
❑ will only eat certain foods presented in a certain way;
❑ will not tolerate being left in anyone else's care;
❑ will not play alone.

You

❑ find no child-care arrangement adequate;
❑ worry endlessly about your child not getting enough of the right things to eat;

❑ worry other children the same age have more advanced verbal and motor skills;

❑ are frequently bringing your child to the pediatrician, only to hear "It's just a cold and it will take its course";

❑ are always saying "Be careful!" "Be careful! You'll get hurt!"

❑ feel every stranger your child encounters intends harm.

Things You Can Do to Let Go of Toddlers and Preschoolers

❑ *Encourage independent play.* We've all heard so much about "quality time" that we think the only proper way to be with our small children is through intensive interaction. While that has its place, it's not the only, or even the best, kind of play a preschooler needs. If you are playing interactively with a preschooler, let your child take the lead, particularly in fantasy play. Be there to help, suggest, and expand but not to intrude your adult wishes and concerns upon a child's play agenda.

When your preschooler is playing by herself and is absorbed in what she's doing, protect the important work your child does through play by protecting her privacy. Resist touching, talking, and getting involved all the time. Let your child know you're there without breaking her concentration.

If she needs help, get her started in an activity, then gradually back off, busying yourself within earshot of your child.

Create optimally safe play spaces: There's no question about it—children beginning to walk, run, swing, and scoot around do tumble and get bumped and bruised. If you can eliminate danger spots (glass tables, hard corners, sharp edges) in your child's play area, your child will be able to play more freely and you will be able to gradually diminish your hawk-eye supervision. Learn first aid and CPR. If you've been telling yourself that signing up for such a class will bring bad luck—wisen up! (While you're at it, get your will written, in case fear of bringing on bad luck has made you postpone that project, too!)

❑ *Encourage skill acquisition.* You may have overprotective tendencies that threaten to limit your child's horizons and may keep your child from learning those skills that could bring him or her a sense of accomplishment and self-esteem throughout his or her life. If so, back off and turn, if you can, to your less fearful spouse or to a child's aunt or uncle. Amy, mother of five-year-old Sandy, explains: "Intellectually, I know Sandy has to be able to learn to ride a bicycle. But I'm too fearful to teach him. So I have my husband, Dan, go out and teach him. I have to stay in the house, mind my own business, and not get involved. I can't even watch. If I were out there, I'd want to hold the bike for him the whole time and keep running with him and never let go. Dan could let go and let Sandy—possibly—fall."

❑ *Encourage separation.* If you are truly fearful that no one will watch your child as well as you do, and feel you must be with him or her always, at the very least, seek out a parent you consider as scrupulous as you and exchange some child care, even if it's for a very short time at first. While Amy feels no one can watch Sandy as well as she can, she does feel she can leave Sandy with her friend Leslie. "Leslie has earned my trust," says Amy. "She's as compulsive, as scrupulous, and as overprotective of her son as I am of mine."

❑ *Keep alert to the way that events from your past are determining the way you may be overprotecting your preschoolers, and recognize the limits to your control over your child.* Janette, a mother of five- and one-year-old sons, lost her younger sister in a car accident when they were teenagers. Today, she wants to protect her boys from the violent images her sons may absorb from television. Janette explains: "My sister's death has given me this sense that I have so

little control over my boys' lives, so little ability to shape and influence them. I live with the fear that when the boys are sixteen and
get into cars—when they're on their own—[an accident] just happens like that, and it can all be over. There's so much pressure from
the media and society on boys to be macho, to impress women
with fast cars. I wish I could keep that macho influence away from
them. In reality, I know that I'll have to deal with having less control
over their lives than I'd wish."

❑ *Cultivate realism in yourself and your child.* Keeping a grip on
fear requires strategy. While John, father of two-year-old Brooke,
acknowledges he worries a lot, he does try to season his worry with
realistic prudence. "My greatest fears are that she will die or be
kidnapped, but I believe those fears stem from my own worry that
I can't control the drunk driver on the road or the lunatic molester
in the mall. I hope I will be able to raise Brooke with a strong sense
of self, of confidence, and fearless pursuit of purpose, coupled with
a very practical sense of realistic caution. Brooke will learn not to
talk to strangers in cars, but hopefully, she will not fear psychos
lurking behind every door. There is a very fine line between necessary caution and hysterical fear, and that is what I will try to
teach her."

If Your Child Is a Toddler or Preschooler, These Are Some of the Protective Decisions You Are Likely to Be Making

Every Day

❑ Should you always insist your child keep to a regular
    schedule, with naps and a set bedtime?
❑ Should you spoon-feed your child or provide an array of
    finger foods?
❑ Will you permit your child to be a picky eater?

❑ When are you and your breast-fed child ready for weaning?
When should a cup replace a bottle?

❑ When is the right time for toilet training?

❑ When do you begin to encourage self-care—brushing teeth,
washing up, getting dressed, putting away toys, bringing
things to the kitchen table?

❑ How do you cope with your child's everyday fears—of the
dark, of loud noises, of dogs, of strangers, of being in new
places? Do you avoid the source of fear or provide ways to
gain security?

Being Alone

❑ Which toys are safe enough to use without your constant
supervision? When will you introduce crayons, clay, paints,
and safety scissors?

❑ When is it time to introduce exciting play equipment, such
as scooters, tricycles, wagons, sandboxes, climbing apparatuses, and wading pools? What requires constant supervision and what doesn't? When is it time for your child to
move into a bed? If your child gets out of bed and wanders
about alone, will he be safe?

❑ Can your child watch TV alone without your being there to
see what's being shown?

❑ Is your child as self-reliant as he or she can sometimes
appear?

Social Life

❑ Do you accept that your child is shy or do you push him or
her to be more sociable? If your child pushes other children
around and is domineering, how do you teach her to get
along better?

❑ If all the other children are going down the slide in the
park, should you urge yours to overcome his or her fears?

Child Care

❑ When is the right time to start? How long a day is too long?

❑ What environment is calm enough? Stimulating enough? When is it time to switch to a different arrangement?

❑ How do you know when your child has settled down in a new environment and it's time for you to leave?

❑ Should you be alarmed if your child cries when you leave? Can you be reassured if the teacher says the crying stopped soon after you left?

Emotional Well-Being

❑ Do you tell your child about exciting things coming up (a holiday, a trip to the grandparents) so he can anticipate them? Do you tell your child in advance about a doctor's appointment or prepare in advance for a medical procedure that will require hospitalization?

❑ Do you explain to your child why you are feeling sad or happy?

❑ Do you allow your child to be sullen or angry, or do you only allow cheerfulness? Are there times and places when blowing off steam is ever appropriate?

7

School-age Children: Ages Six Through Twelve

As children go off to school, we become further challenged as their protectors. For larger parts of the day, we are physically disconnected from them and cannot always know what they're experiencing. They are touched and molded by what they see and hear from teachers, peers, television, and movies—and we can't monitor all their influences.

We're tugged this way and that. School-age children want to blend in with their friends and be liked, and while we want them to be part of the group, too, we don't want them to forget who they are or what they've been taught. We want them to be able to fend for themselves, yet we want to be there as their advocates when they need us.

With the urges to restrain and release compelling us with equal intensity, we can feel stuck in the middle, between the push and the pull. Arthur, the father of seven-year-old Naceo, explains: "On sunlit mornings, I'll wake up knowing that the best thing for Naceo is to push him into the world—let him be free, rough and tumble. But I can become so scared for him," Arthur says quietly, waving two sets of fingers crossed for good luck in the air. "Naceo is now old enough to ride his bike in the street. We were out bicycling together, and he was about to go down the hill before me. Alone! On his own! My God, I thought, a car could come out of nowhere. I knew I had done everything to make his ride safe—I made him wear a helmet, I picked a quiet neighborhood with big, wide streets and few cars—and we've done this so many times together. But I thought, Some 'un-miracle' could happen, and Naceo could be struck down. I had to let him go down, though." Arthur is convinced that a parent who protects too much makes a child submissive. He believes overprotection is a form of control that's disguised as caring but is, in fact, aggressive and sadistic. "Naceo was looking to me for his sense of independence," says Arthur, who, with his heart in his stomach, stood at the top of the hill that day and watched Naceo go down alone.

Protecting Children in Cities

Parents raising school-age children in big cities stay continually perched on their toes, daily negotiating and renegotiating when to hold on and when to let go. Kayla and Lucas, married musicians who live in New York City, are constantly considering the protective issues that face their school-age sons, Nikki, seven, and Clem, twelve. While they acknowledge that city kids are expected to be more savvy than their rural and suburban peers, they wonder how much more risk is wise for them to encounter.

Violence

Kayla and Lucas have every reason to fear the boys could be shot to death by a stray bullet. "When the boys were tiny," Kayla recalls, "I was strolling down Amsterdam Avenue with Nikki in my back carrier and Clem holding my hand when a bullet crossed our path and shattered a bank window. Another time, Lucas was in the grocery store with the boys when the window was shattered by a bullet, and glass flew all over them. Most recently, we were all out on Broadway shopping and suddenly got caught in a police shoot-out. The police had their guns drawn and came running out and screamed at us, 'Down! Get back!' " After each of these experiences, Lucas and Kayla ask each other, "How do we protect kids when we can't protect them? How do we prepare for the stray bullet?"

Because Kayla and Lucas love city living and want to communicate that affection to their boys, they have decided they will not live in fear or let fear hole them up indoors. "There is no way we can protect a child from stray bullets, just as there is no way we can protect a child from a cold. But there are enough other forms of danger we can protect a child from," says Lucas.

Kayla and Lucas began teaching their boys to be careful from an early age, so that the rules for safety would be well internalized. "We don't have to remind them what to do all the time," says Lucas, "if they can tell *themselves* what they ought to be doing. When we go outside, they've been trained to stay close to us so we can grab them out of harm's way. We trained them to leave any park by sundown, no matter whom they're with. If it's an uncle or a sitter, they're to say, 'I have to go home now.' "

Rehearsals

Periodically, the boys must rehearse what they would do if they are bothered by strangers, and if they hear of classmates who were harassed or had a narrow escape, they are encouraged to consider what they might have done in the same situation. When the boys were younger, Lucas was especially concerned they would become separated from him on the subway. "They liked to dart into the subway car. If one of them got in and the door closed before I got in, I'd have no way of stopping the train. Since the boys were two years old, we've taught them that if they get on a subway car by mistake without a parent and the door closed, they are to get off at the next stop, go over to the token booth, and tell the attendant 'I'm lost,' and wait until the parent arrived. For years, every time we'd walk down the stairs to the subway, I'd say, 'What do you do if we get separated?' As if I were pressing a button on a tape recorder, they'd spout back the right response."

The Process of Negotiating a Child's Physical Freedom

Kayla had been reluctant to let the boys go outside to play without supervision, even though their friends could do this. She wondered if she was being overprotective. She was aware that she, like her own parents, tends to think about what could go wrong rather than what could go right. While her decision to hold on felt appropriate for the time being, she knew that eventually she would have to let both boys go more and more.

Eventually came sooner than she thought.

When Clem turned nine, Lucas told Kayla he felt the time had come to let go of Clem some more—the red lights would have to start switching to green lights. Lucas has typically been the parent who is more eager to let go. Kayla speculates why this is so: "Lucas was raised by his parents with benign neglect; he has this sense that you can do what you like and things will turn out okay."

The moment for change happened when Clem announced he wanted to walk the two blocks home alone from his violin lesson. He was humiliated that children younger than he had greater mobility.

Lucas led the way as they worked together through this decision. He began by talking to parents of the other violin students. Several were letting their children, the same age as Clem or even younger, walk home alone. Lucas then observed young children carrying musical instruments who were obviously going alone to or from lessons in the neighborhood. He tried to evaluate how secure they appeared. While a child with a violin case might look like easier prey than one carrying a hockey stick, the young violinists that Lucas saw on the street looked confident enough to him.

Lucas pulled together his thoughts: Clem himself wanted more freedom and responsibility; he had the right skills for crossing streets and avoiding strangers; and he had demonstrated he could use this knowledge confidently. Next, the environment was sufficiently secure. Clem was born and raised in the area and most neighborhood merchants along the street knew him. Surely they'd scold him if he was getting out of line or protect him if he was being threatened.

Gradually Relaxing the Vigilance

Once Lucas felt confident it was a good idea, Kayla was willing to give it a try. It was a decision she could live with, without feeling sick to her stomach. They let Clem walk home from violin lessons, except for in the middle of winter when it got dark so early. At first, Lucas or Kayla would stand inside a shop and peek as Clem walked home, just to satisfy themselves that he could make it. Later, they peeked from their apartment window. Finally, he just showed up at the door and they began to take his walk home for granted.

I Say He Can Go . . . I Say He Can't

Parents who generally cooperate on making protective decisions will not always see eye to eye. When Clem turned ten, Lucas felt it was time for him to take his monthly trips to the orthodontist by bus alone.

His procedure had been the same as usual—speaking to other parents, observing children the same age, evaluating Clem's skills, listening to Clem's own desires.

This time, Kayla refused to give her blessing. While most facts Lucas gathered indicated Clem could make this trip alone, the thought of him doing it still made Kayla feel sick. It was

Clem's personality, in particular, that made her hesitate: "I could picture him missing his stop, getting lost, and not knowing what to do," says Kayla. "Nikki's different: If he got lost, he'd know whom to approach to get rescued."

For the time being, traveling by bus alone remains a yellow light situation for Kayla and Lucas. Regularly, Lucas has been telling Kayla, "You think Clem won't make it, but he can. There are age-appropriate times for kids to get around alone in this city. We have to let Clem begin to separate from us."

Indeed, Kayla knows Lucas has a point. But when Lucas makes blanket statements about letting go, she wants to draw upon maternal prerogative and tell him "I didn't give birth to these children to have them die somewhere!" or find some other emotional dart that works for a while to buy time. "Lucas is ready and Clem is ready, but I'm not," Kayla maintains. "I need more time to think it through and get used to the idea."

Separate Your Issues from Your Child's

Our awful memories from our own school days prompt us to be poised—perhaps over poised—to protect our children from the very miseries we endured. Karen, mother of Emma, who is in the third grade, knows she struggles to separate Emma's reality from what she calls her own "issues."

"I get hyper when I think a teacher is being mean or cruel or unjust to Emma," Karen confesses. From the first to the third grade, Karen had a certain teacher who robbed her of her self-esteem. By the time she finished third grade, Karen had become a terror, unable to learn. "What awful repercussions that teacher has had on my life," Karen says. "My whole sense of self derives from those years with her. To this day, I don't trust easily. I don't trust strangers, I don't trust babysitters, I surely don't trust teachers."

Consequently, Karen stands on guard for Emma to be sure

her teachers don't destroy her self-esteem or keep her from learning properly. "Just one mediocre teacher who doesn't like my child could ruin her life."

Karen knows there is no necessary connection between her past and her daughter's present. Still, she can't keep herself from getting overinvolved with every little detail of Emma's schooling. She grills Emma to be sure she's being treated fairly, even though she has no reason to be suspicious. When she hears anything that could potentially turn into a problem she gets knots in her stomach until she goes to school to voice her concerns. "It's like an anxiety attack: The thing I'm worried about for Emma consumes me and my whole body has this nervous feeling."

Getting a Grip

How does Karen try to keep some perspective? Given her tendency to confuse Emma's issues with her own, given her tendency to be physically consumed by anxiety, she knows she needs some strategy and has found a five-step procedure that works for her.

"Number one: I try not to get hysterical. I take some deep breaths from my diaphragm and slowly let them go, like in natural childbirth.

"Number two: I talk myself into being more reasonable. I'll ask, 'What's really going on here? Whose issue is this, mine or Emma's?' Because I know I can't always distinguish.

"Number three: I'll talk this through with my husband. He has his own pet peeves, but we're pretty good at not feeding into each other's craziness. I'll tell him, 'I think Emma's teacher is picking on her.' He's heard this before a million times, so he'll ask, 'What makes you say so?' Then I'll give him the evidence I have so far. Only if he thinks I have something to go on, he'll say, 'Go ahead and find out if your fears are based in reality.'

"Number four: I start collecting information, first from

Emma. I check with other parents, and of course I check with the school.

"Once, Emma's gym teacher gave her an N for 'needs improvement' in behavior. I asked Emma what was going on. She shrugged and didn't want to talk about it, which made me nervous. None of the parents I spoke with had any complaints or concerns about this new gym teacher, so that was a good sign, I guess. I telephoned the gym teacher because I wanted to know what was going on. Why did he give Emma an N when none of her other teachers ever remarked about her having a behavior problem? The gym teacher said Emma started out being cooperative at the beginning of the year, but now she's bouncing off the walls just like the other kids. The teacher didn't think it was a discipline problem; he thought it had something to do with Emma wanting to fit in.

"Finally, comes reflection: I sat down and tried to be as objective as a parent can be, which is not easy. I asked myself, Could this be true? Was my child capable of doing what this teacher said? I tried to reconstruct what was going on in gym. Could the teacher have been making it all up? Could it be something he was doing to make all the kids bounce off the walls? Was it my daughter's fault if he can't control a class and the kids sense it? Once I asked myself all these questions and answered them as best I could, I pretty much decided that the situation the gym teacher described was real and could be dealt with. It seemed as if Emma really was casting about for ways to fit in. Of course, I didn't think giving her an N was any way to deal with it, and I told that to the teacher."

Karen admits her step-by-step approach only works if the situation hasn't yet made her hysterical. "If I suspected Emma were being abused physically by a teacher, there's no way I could go about calmly breathing or collecting evidence."

Trusting Others Who Are in Charge of Your Children

Karen's difficulty in trusting others to watch out for her daughter as scrupulously as she would herself extends beyond school teachers. For instance, she won't give Emma blanket permission to go on all of the summer activities planned by the YMCA day camp. She's nixed some trips after thought and investigation. Here's how Karen goes about working through such a decision.

"First of all, I accept I will have to let Karen do many things I'm not 100 percent comfortable with, simply because I know that at this point in her life, I need to let go some. When I first sent Emma to the Y day-camp, I checked out the things that concerned me. What was the ratio of children to swimming counselors, children to life guards, and how intense was the supervision? Were the life guards serious adults or were they college kids on break who were preening themselves?

"Next, I weigh the various factors, keeping in sight what effect my decision will have on Emma. Last month, for example, the Y was taking the kids to a sports park. When I learned the kids were going off in pairs and would not be with counselors the entire time, it didn't seem safe enough. Emma isn't sports crazy and she didn't have her heart set on going, so I didn't feel as if I was pulling the rug out from under her feet by having her stay home. She asked me if she could go, she argued with me for a while, and then it was over. Why did she stop arguing so fast? I think she understood how seriously I was concerned about the dangers and knew I wasn't going to change my mind. In the end, she was just as happy to go to the mall for school clothes with her aunt.

"This past week, the Y was taking the kids to a planetarium. I knew Emma had been dying to go because she'd talked about it all summer. I kept calling the director of the Y to check out the specific arrangements for supervision. On this trip, the kids weren't being allowed to run free—they were going in groups of four, with a counselor. When the bus for the planetarium left the Y, Emma was on it. I let her go because I felt she would be watched and because I told her 50 million times not to talk to strangers and to keep her counselor in eyeshot. I knew Emma was aware of the dangers she might encounter and that she would use good judgment." While Karen wasn't 100 percent sure this really was a green-light decision, she did believe Emma would be safe. (This story, by the way, has a bittersweet ending: Even though Emma was eventually allowed to go to the planetarium, we might well wonder how freely she was able to enjoy herself once she got there.)

Kids with Special Needs

Raising school-age children with special needs brings its own set of challenges. Even if your child does not have special needs, I think you'll be as touched by this story as I was.

Sophia, the mother of Jed, a young man born without legs, recalls that from the moment Jed was born, she was struck with the thought that her son might never be independent. "All parents have a problem separating from their children, so I knew the more dependent Jed was on me, the more difficult it would be for him to ever separate. I was literally his legs, carrying him around for so many years. How would he ever have the confidence to leave me?"

Sophia directed every day toward preparing Jed for independence. If he said he wanted a glass for juice or asked her to run up and get his backpack, she told him to do it himself. When he got his artificial legs, she insisted that he use them every day, from ten in the morning till two in the afternoon. "People would tell me I was too hard on Jed. It would have been so much easier for me to say 'You don't have to put your legs on,' but I didn't give in. Jed needed to be able to get around and, eventually, to go off on his own."

At the same time, Sophia wanted to protect Jed from what other people said. It pained her to see children whispering in a corner and pointing. "Please, God," she'd pray, "don't let other children make fun of him." At public beaches, kids inevitably circled Jed and stared. "Fortunately," says Sophia, "we could afford to go to a private beach, so Jed wouldn't be subjected to so many questions and so much scrutiny. That was one way my husband and I protected Jed; otherwise, it was too much for all of us to bear."

Sophia had always taught Jed to deal with people's questions courteously and directly. "People don't mean harm, but children say unkind things and adults are appallingly stupid. We told Jed it was incumbent upon him to help them. We told him to say 'I wear artificial legs.' When Jed was six, I was carrying him in a pharmacy and a man said, 'You're such a big boy, how come you let your mother carry you?' I just lost it then. I told the man, 'Mister, why don't you mind your own business?' But then Jed just said, 'Because I wear artificial legs.' Jed had responded to the man the way I should have. The man said, 'Oh, I'm so sorry.' I said, 'I'm sorry, too. I apologize.' Now, whenever Jed goes into an elevator and people ask if he broke his legs skiing, he tells them he wears artificial legs and people start apologizing. Then Jed says reassuringly, 'You don't have to be sorry. I'm fine.'"

Protecting Doesn't Require Shielding as Much as Forethought

When Jed started kindergarten, Sophia needed to find a way to introduce him to the other children on the first day of school. The principal, Sophia, and her husband created a plan. Sophia recalls: "There was to be an opening program for children and their parents. We decided the teacher would ask the children to each tell how they were different. Beforehand, we told Jed he was going to say he wore artificial legs and these were his crutches. We told him the children would want to see his legs, because they'd be painfully curious, and he was to show them. I knew Jed could get through this. Still, I didn't sleep all the night before.

"One little girl got up and said, 'I have a little thing on my heinie, but no on can see it.' One boy said he couldn't see well so he wore glasses. Jed got up and said, 'I wear artificial legs.' The teacher asked, 'Can the children see them?' Jed didn't say anything. Of course, I was dying. For me, it was so horrible. But Jed lifted up his trouser leg and one at a time the children touched, asking, 'You mean you don't feel that?' Jed said he didn't. That was the end of it. Jed went to this school system through twelfth grade and there were no questions and no staring and no making fun. As it happened, Jed was very popular; he has more friends than the church. But if he hadn't been accepted, it would have been because he was a creepy kid and not because he wore artificial legs.

"That morning was very hard to live through. It was the right thing to do, but it killed me. Just recently, I got a call from a woman whose son was born without an arm. She had heard from the principal that we handled Jed's first day of school in a special way and wanted to know what we had done. Her instincts were good: She knew she had to plan ahead to protect her son in some way. So I told her what we did. She said, 'No way! If you think I'm going to let all those kids touch my child—no way!' I thought to myself, with her attitude, her child is going to have a hard time making it."

Some Signs that You May Be Overprotecting a School-age Child

Your Child

❑ usually refuses to play with peers and prefers being with you—and always in the very same room;

- ❏ usually refuses to go to a friend's house or birthday party unless you come too and promise to stay the whole time;
- ❏ depends on you to resolve his difficulties with siblings, friends, and teachers;
- ❏ claims he cannot do assigned homework or a school project unless you are present and involved every step of the way;
- ❏ prefers sleeping in your room even though he has his own;
- ❏ depends on you to pick out clothes and get dressed;
- ❏ depends on you for entertainment and companionship;
- ❏ is unusually clingy, not just in new situations or with unfamiliar people who make him feel insecure, but most of the time.

You

- ❏ are at your child's school volunteering so often that others assume you work there;
- ❏ are the only parent in your child's grade who still escorts her to school or waits with her at the bus stop;
- ❏ find something wrong with just about any friend your child picks, and when you meet the parents, they are not to your liking either;
- ❏ are quick to justify why you must do things for your child that her peers are doing for themselves, such as cleaning up, buttering toast, brushing hair, bathing;
- ❏ are quick to find reasons to prohibit any age-appropriate physical challenges, such as ice-skating, skateboarding, or roller-skating, which might end in scrapes and black-and-blue marks;
- ❏ have been so emphatic about warning your child about dangerous strangers that he is terrified of anyone unfamiliar;
- ❏ continue to be solicitous after your child has recovered from an illness, remain concerned about the recurrence of

symptoms, and impose restrictions on activities long after the illness has clearly passed;

❑ have a heightened sense of responsibility—you feel it is your job to stand in the way of harm to your child wherever he is.

Things You Can Do to Let Go of School-age Children

❑ *Notice the responsibilities and skills your child's peers have been given.* If peers are helping with housekeeping by emptying their own garbage cans, making their beds, helping with meal preparation, or clearing the dinner table, can your child do these things as well? If other children are packing their own school bags and checking their memo pads to see if they have everything they need, could your child do this too? If your child's peers are all riding two-wheel bikes and are able to swim with their faces in the water, could your child do these things or does he or she know how to? (Note: Your child may prefer to learn these things in private: If all the eleven-year-olds are swimming and diving and your child can't even swim, he may prefer taking private lessons rather than being seen in public taking a class with the six-year-olds.) If a disability prevents your child from taking on specific physical challenges, is there some alternative way your child can feel he or she is participating? (One twelve-year-old boy with a heart condition was not allowed to run or ride a bicycle. His doctor encouraged his parents to buy him a little moped so he could keep up with his friends and experience the thrill of movement.)

❑ *Pay attention to the risks your child's peers are permitted to take.* May his peers walk to school in groups and cross at the light? Are they permitted to walk to each other's houses in the neighborhood during the day? Are they allowed to walk their dogs, go sledding down the big slope in the park? If your child knows the proper safety skills and can respond to danger predictably, is there some reason why he can't take on the same risks as his peers? Are your prohibitions giving your child the sense that he or she is more delicate, more accident-prone, and less agile and coordinated than his or her peers? If your child is fearful about physical risks, do you feed into them and confirm them? If this is your youngest child, are you allowing him to mature at the same rate as older siblings, or are you perpetuating the child's babyhood?

❑ *Listen closely to what your child is asking you to permit or teach her to do.* Acknowledge and respect your child's desires to be more grown-up and more competent—even if it makes you sad to be losing your "baby." If your child asks permission to go to a movie that will be scarier or sadder than you are comfortable with, he or she may want to do more than keep up with what's hot: She may want to test out his or her ability to confront stronger emotions. That doesn't mean sending your child off to the latest Clint Eastwood movie, but it could mean letting her see PG movies like *Free Willy* or *Home Alone*. If, for instance, your child is asking for in-line skates, she may want far more than a coveted toy: She may want to feel good about herself as she skates down the sidewalk in a line with her friends. So, when your child makes a request, consider what motive for personal or social maturity may be behind it.

❑ *Take note of how self-reliant your child is compared to his peers.* Discover ways you can send the message to your child that you trust him to take care of himself and make the right decisions when you are not there. For instance, if your child is reasonably consistent about going to bed on time, on a weekend night you may want to tell him, "You can read or play quietly in your room until you're tired. I trust you won't stay up too late." Or if it's very cold out and you're all going sledding, tell your child, "You'll need three layers of clothes. Decide what you think will work best and be ready to go in fifteen minutes." Or at mealtime, try "You don't need to finish everything on your plate, but I don't want you to be hungry again in an hour." Or if you're going on a trip, give your child guidelines for what to pack and hand him his own suitcase. Then let him do the picking and packing himself.

❑ *Discover what you are doing for your child that she can do for herself, even if she doesn't do it as well as you.* That could include ordering her own food in a restaurant, shopping for school clothes or presents in a store, or making all or part of a school lunch. She'll make mistakes at first, but she'll wisen up with experience.

❑ *If your child is quarreling with a friend, wait before you intervene.* Unless someone might be injured, give the children a chance to resolve their difficulties on their own before you or the other parent mediate.

❑ *Remember that school is your child's territory.* If your child wants to share what happened in school, great, but don't expect him to tell you everything that's going on. If your child is complaining that a teacher is unfair or mean or picking on her, wait and see if the issue resolves itself before you intervene. While you want to be on your child's side, resist continually criticizing his teachers and siding with him against them. Help your child to see things from the teacher's point of view. For instance, if your child complains that his teacher never calls on him, you might say, "Even though you're the first to raise your hand, your teacher may not be ignoring you when she doesn't call on you. She knows you have the right answer and she wants to see if the other children know. That's the only way she can tell who needs more help before she goes on." Of course, if you get a sense that a teacher is truly malicious or painfully inept, you'll get involved and step in.

❑ *Help your child to find the solutions to her own problems.* A parent's overeagerness to solve school problems can sometimes elevate a nonissue ninto a big deal. If the issue persists, first help your child solve the problem by herself by considering all the ways you can help her be her own best advocate. If she's sitting next to a pesky kid, she can ask the teacher to let her change places. If she doesn't get what's going on in science, she can ask for extra help herself before you ask for her or complain to the principal that the science teacher is going too fast.

❑ *You will know when the situation is too complex for your child to handle alone.* For instance, you would obviously get involved yourself if your child weren't getting the proper supplementary services for special needs, such as speech, remediation, or enrichment. You'd intervene if you felt inappropriate material was being included in your child's permanent record or if she was punished or suspended unfairly. You'd take on the school, even go so far as to file a lawsuit, if there were unsafe physical conditions, such as the presence of lead-contaminated dust or asbestos. You'd intervene if night after night your child complained that her teacher was harassing or humiliating her. In a case like that, you know it's time to call the school, send a note to the teacher, arrange to come in for a meeting, or mobilize other parents.

❑ *Maintain times and places for your child to be comfortably alone.* When you are home together, pay attention to how much time your child spends in the same room as you're in. If he is always with you, try gradually extending the times that you are each busy in different rooms. Teach your child that he has a right to privacy, as does every member of the family. If your door is closed, your child should knock; if your child's door is closed, you too should knock. Be cautious not to impose privacy ("Go to your room!") as a punishment.

❑ *Try not to disapprove of the friends your child chooses.* Let your child select his own friends, even if the relationships make no sense to you. Every friend your child makes in grade school isn't going to be a soul mate for life. For example, a quiet child may choose to chum around with a boisterous mischief maker because the friendship lets him experience other ways of being. Unless you intervene or make a fuss, friendships that don't make sense usually fade away.

Children seek out what they need in friendships. Unless the friend is obviously trouble, such as a child who is taking advantage of yours or one who is coercing him or her to take life-threatening risks, try to trust your child's own friendship-seeking instincts.

❑ *Encourage your child to feel secure when separate from you.* When your child arranges play dates, encourage him to play at the other children's houses as often as he plays at your house, even if your child insists that your house is "more fun" or that he doesn't like his friend's house. You'll know when a playmate's turf is truly too unpleasant: perhaps there's an impending divorce, a menacing dog, an older child around who taunts and torments his siblings. If a friend or relative you trust invites your child to go to the movies or on an outing, consider saying yes instead of immediately finding numerous logistical reasons to nix the invitation. If your spouse, whom you consider less protective than you, decides to go off alone with your child, see if you can encourage the outing without offering warnings, precautions, and subtle discouragement. Try limiting your parting comments to "Have a good time!" Take up grandma and grandpa's offer to watch your child while you go away for the evening or the weekend. If your child is going on a school trip, don't always be the parent who volunteers to go along as class mother or class father; let your child have the opportunity to negotiate the outing alone. Without you there, she'll have to carry her own money to buy a drink, pick out a souvenir by herself, and be responsible for keeping up with the group. If friends invite you to dinner, don't be so quick to ask if you can bring the kids. Consider saying yes to an evening social event you are invited to, even though it will be difficult to find a sitter. By the way: When *was* the last time you went out at night? Make up a reason to get a sitter and go out, even if it's for a long walk or cup of coffee. By refusing to hire sitters, you encourage your child to believe that unless he's with you, he's in danger.

Beginning the Process of Letting Go

When our children become school-age, many of us first notice just how overprotective we've become. If, at this point, you discover you've been overprotecting and would like to revise your protective approach, you'll want the letting go to be gradual.

In the past you may have

- ○ prepared your child's school lunch because you felt it wouldn't be nutritious enough if she made it herself;
- ○ felt your child wouldn't be responsible enough to keep an eye on a younger sibling;
- ○ laid out your child's clothes because you didn't trust he could match his clothes to the weather and to the demands of the occasion; or
- ○ typed out your child's reports because you felt it was less of a burden for you, or because you felt the report would have a better shot at a good grade if it were neatly presented.

If all of a sudden you announce to your son, for example, that from now on he is to make his lunch or watch his little sister or pick out his own clothes or type his own papers—possibly adding, "You're a big boy now! You have to learn to be responsible for yourself! I'm tired of having to do everything for you, waiting on you hand and foot!"—chances are your child will feel confused, betrayed, and deprived of the accustomed demonstrations of your love and care.

What did I do wrong to have all these added responsibilities thrown in my face? he may wonder. "Why am I being punished?" he might say. "It's not my fault that I never did these things for myself. You never let me do any of these things on my own. I thought you *wanted* to do them for me, because when you do it, you do it right. Don't you love me anymore?"

Don't be angry at your child if he or she balks at a change in the status quo. Change, even change for the better, is confusing and disconcerting at first; any break in routine throws us off and lowers our comfort level. While your child will eventually feel proud and confident about being able to take care of herself, this will not be apparent at the beginning. This is particularly true if a child feels she is being left to fend for or herself, with neither the skills nor the confidence to succeed.

Tips for Making Changes

○ *Increase responsibility.* To keep family relations on a more even keel as you work together through these transitions, increase your child's responsibilities step by step. Make sure that your child perceives the new skills and responsibilities as neither rewards nor punishments: They are just the natural activities of children his age, as natural as the move from crawling to walking.

○ *Foster skill development.* Let your child gradually master the new skills he or she needs to catch up with his peers. Just because your child's watched you make school lunches and eaten them doesn't mean he or she understands the concept of a balanced meal. Just because your child has watched you make tuna fish sandwiches doesn't mean he will know you need a tablespoon for the mayonnaise, a fork to flake the tuna, and a cutting board to protect the Formica counter. If you have always made your child's lunches without consulting him, begin by asking your child what he would like you to make or which choices are preferred. (The hard part of lunch preparation is not spreading the peanut butter on the bread, it's figuring out "What, given what we have in the fridge, do I feel like making?") From there, allow your child to take over a portion of the preparation as you work side by side: While you fix the main course, have your child wash the fruit, wrap up some cookies, and pick out a juice box. When this has become habitual, let your child tackle the main course, under your supervision at first. Teach him the proper and safest way to use kitchen equipment, beginning with the least risky items. Prepare the meal at night and not in the morning: Without the pressure of having to get to the school bus on time, you'll be less apt to take over the operations yourself or fret that it's taking longer or getting messier than it would have if you had done it alone. Hold off on chastising your child for spills and mistakes. Your child knows when he has goofed and will probably get it right next time.

○ *Rehearse contingency plans.* Once the skills are well in place, talk through contingency plans for unexpected occurrences. What if there's a fire in the toaster oven? What if the phone or doorbell rings while you're cooking? What if you cut or burn your finger?

○ *Go step by step.* How might this step-by-step approach work if you wanted to encourage an older child to take responsibility for younger siblings? Obviously, if your ten-year-old son has never baby-sat for his two-year-old sister, you wouldn't just announce one day, "I'm leaving you in charge." Let your son watch and be responsible for his little sister while you're home but too busy to take care of her yourself. Next, put him in charge while you're outside washing the car. Then, put him in charge while you're over at the neighbors talking. Go over the safety precautions he should keep in mind and rehearse scenarios that could arise and solutions for dealing with them ("If your sister wakes up from her nap crying for her pacifier and you can't find it, there are spares in the kitchen drawer. If she wakes up cranky, what do you think might entertain her? Your old Sesame Street tape?").

Emotional Overprotection

So far, we've focused primarily on the physical and social ways school-age children are overprotected. We can't forget another way that children in this age group are frequently overprotected, and that is in the arena of emotional overprotection.

We overprotect emotionally when we bend over backward to shield our children from knowing unpleasant feelings, sadness, disappointments, frights, worries, and serious concerns. Where do we draw the line? Obviously no parent wants to subject a child to emotions that a child has no business having to deal with. For instance, no school-age child needs to agonize over the details of a grandparent's painful or hopeless cancer treatment. No child deserves to be subjected to all the stresses a parent feels if he or she has become unemployed and is facing enormous financial pressures.

On the other hand, if a grandparent is sick and dying, a school-age child has as much right as any other member of the family to know the truth about what's going on, to visit, pray, prepare, feel anger, and say good-bye.

If mom has been out of work for three months, a child has the right to know why mom is hovering over the telephone. While a child ideally shouldn't have to worry about where her next meal is coming from, if a family is economically strapped, a child should be able to understand what the belt-tightening is all about and, if the child's old enough, maybe help in her own way.

You May Be Emotionally Overprotecting Your Child if You

○ don't tell your child about a dentist or doctor appointment until minutes before to spare her the anxiety, and you give no hint that the visit may include a shot or other invasive procedure because you fear your child will get all worked up;

○ hide the fact that grandparents or other close friends and relatives are ill; if they are terminally ill, you censor all facts and conceal your own emotions; and if there are funerals, you keep your child far away from all mourning rituals;

○ postpone telling your child about an impending divorce for as long as possible;

○ attempt to protect your child's self-esteem by finding excuses to dismiss her failures (such as by saying your child performed poorly on a test only because the test and the teacher who wrote it were stupid and unfair, and in doing so, you may inadvertently teach her that failure is not acceptable);

○ keep your child from feeling disappointment by always finding alternative ways to "make it up" to her;

○ keep your child from feeling guilty by hiding the fact that his actions have consequences (for example, you omit telling your daughter that if she had remembered to shut the back door when she came in, the cat would not have run away);

○ make up stories to protect your child from truths you can't bear to see him face (for example, you switch a live goldfish for a dead one so your child will not have to suffer loss; or you substitute the "We gave our dog to a lovely family with a farm in the country" story for the truth);

○ never show sadness or disappointment in front of your child, because you believe if he saw you "fall apart," he would lose his sense of security; or

○ never argue with your partner or raise your voices in front of your child because you don't want him to imagine that your disagreements are more serious.

Barbara Hyatte Pressley, a clinical social worker, offers this advice as we draw the line between subjecting our school-age children to emotions they can appropriately handle and protecting them from emotions that would be inappropriate.

"In trying to shield children from difficult emotions so they don't become unduly distressed, parents end up scaring the children even more by their silence and their white lies. In fact, the parent's worst fear—that the child will become distressed—happens." Even when school-age children are "kept in the dark," they are such good sleuths that they generally know something is going on. Unfortunately, they think the bad things that are happening may be their fault. If parents are fighting, children think they are the cause of the strife. If children pick up whispers about illness, they think it's their mothers or fathers who will die and leave them. They imagine that they, in some way, have caused the illness. They fear that they will be abandoned. Children Pressley treats whose parents are divorcing or are facing terminal illness often say to her, "My parents didn't want to tell me, but I knew; I saw Daddy crying" (or "I saw Mommy yelling").

"Whatever is going on in your family—sickness, divorce, whatever—can be explained on a kid's level," says Pressley, who often uses story books in her practice to address the difficult emotional experiences children encounter. "You cannot refuse to talk about the situation with your child and think it will go away. Spare the gory details, tell them only what they need to know, be willing to repeat the information over and over again so they can absorb it, and assure them they have not the caused the problem. Because children are so afraid they did something wrong, their experience of hearing what's actually going on is often relief! 'Is this what's happening? That I can handle!' Kids are much stronger than we imagine. Unlike adults, who will learn some bad news and obsess about it, kids can compartmentalize. They can put the news aside for a while and go play. Kids don't fully absorb the shock all at once. A child will learn his grandmother has died and then a few weeks later will ask, 'When is Nanna coming back?' "

When parents shield their children from having an emotional life, they steal their children's legitimate right to experience the whole range of feelings. That includes hard emotions, such as sadness, anger, loneliness, disappointment, or nervous anticipation. There is nothing wrong when a child has a nervous stomach on the first day of school; most of us still feel that way when we are about to embark on something new and unfamiliar. There's nothing wrong when a child is disappointed if a long-awaited day at the beach gets rained out. "Parents are quick to label certain emotions as bad, off-limits, or dangerous," says Pressley. "Parents distinguish them from the emotions they consider good and safe for children, such as happiness, love and excitement. For a child to develop into a adult who has empathy, she needs to have been exposed to the whole range of human emotions." Protecting a child from having off-limit feelings restricts her from being fully human, making her feel she must avoid certain emotions because her parents have indicated they would overwhelm her. Such a practice encourages a child to stay clear of all situations that might arouse those forbidden emotions.

For instance, when a child is expecting a friend to come play but the friend cancels out at the last moment, some parents will rush around to come up with a compensating activity to keep their child from feeling even a moment's disappointment. "If Marissa can't come at the last minute, and your child feels rotten about it," says Pressley, "allow her to express how rotten it feels. Acknowledge her disappointment. Let her feel her own pain. Encourage her to come up with a constructive response to her situation, instead of providing one for her that will be distracting. Let her be the one to decide, 'Maybe I could call up Sharon and see if she can play.'" If she learns how to improvise, she'll have the courage to make plans, even though they might flop and leave her temporarily disappointed.

If You Have a School-age Child, These Are Some of the More Common Protective Decisions You're Likely to Be Making

Being Alone

❑ Can your child play alone outside?

❑ Can your child stay at home with a sibling, a friend, or all alone? And when? During the day? Until you come home from work? At night? When you are down the block? When you are farther away?

❑ Can your child who is home alone be trusted to keep busy, stay away from the stove, deal with phone calls and doorbells, call 911 for emergencies, deal with cuts and bruises, respond to a fire or thunderstorm?

Traveling

❑ Can your child walk or bicycle to school? To a friend's house?

❑ Can your child wait at the bus stop alone?

❑ Can your child go to the playground with friends? Go downtown, to the movies, to the library, to the mall? Can you send your child on errands to the neighbors or to the market?

❑ Can your child take a bus, train, or plane to a different city, where she will be met? Will your child be able to handle herself if the bus or train is delayed or rerouted?

❑ Can your child take a city bus alone or with friends?

❑ Can your child go on an excursion with a class or youth group?

Social Life

☐ Can your child sleep over at a friend's?

☐ Can your child go to a bowling alley, pool, beach house, or tourist attraction with a friend's family?

☐ Can your child go to sleep-away camp?

☐ Can your child play with a child whose family has ethical or religious beliefs that differ from yours?

School

☐ Are you satisfied that the school has taken the appropriate precautions to prevent violence? Is discipline handled appropriately?

☐ Are other children keeping your child from learning?

☐ Is your child's teacher competent? Is the teacher sensitive to your child's special needs?

☐ Has your child been placed at the right level so he is challenged but not frustrated?

☐ Do you limit the after-school activities your child participates in in an attempt to reduce stress? Will you arrange for enrichment activities to help your child fill up his time wisely and focus on special talents?

Equipment and Machines

☐ Can your child shower or take a bath without supervision?

☐ Can your child use the oven, microwave, popcorn popper, blender, or hairdryer without supervision? What about the dishwasher, vacuum cleaner, electric garage door, VCR?

☐ Can your child ride a two-wheeler, skate, ski, sled, skateboard, go on a roller coaster, waterslide, canoe, sailboat? If the answer is yes, what level of supervision do you demand?

Emotional Well-Being

❑ Should you censor the TV shows and movies your child watches or the books she reads because you think they're too violent, too sexually explicit, or too frightening?

❑ How much do you tell your child about real family problems concerning health, relationships, and financial security?

8

Teenagers

Protection May Be More Difficult
than Before . . .

How much easier it was to protect young children, however overwhelming it seemed at the time. We would hear that old folk expression, "Little children, little troubles; big children, big troubles," and, red-eyed and dragging, say "Huh?" How could we handle more than we already had on our plates?

With young children, we felt we could name and anticipate most dangers. They were concrete, specific: a glass table, a match, a staircase, an oven. We'd scan an environment for potential danger, making a new room kid-safe in minutes.

Once we trained a young child to keep away or we set up protective barriers, we knew we had done our job—at least until the next leap in curiosity and mobility. We knew we'd have to protect differently at each new stage, but we could more or less predict what was coming up and keep one step ahead. We knew the glass coffee table that posed no threat to our infant would become dangerous as soon as he toddled about using the furniture as a support.

With our younger teens, we still retain some of the control we once had. "When my children were thirteen, fourteen," says Jan, "I'd say, 'You absolutely may not do this!' or 'Be careful!'

I assumed the children would listen to my rules and warnings, and they would be safe." Such control can go out the window with older teens. "My children are nineteen and twenty now," says Jan, "and my anxiety has heightened. I can do nothing to protect them. I try to hold my tongue. All my anxiety is internalized." Author Robb Forman Dew depicts a parent of an older teen as she confronts her powerlessness.

> *She no longer had any power to protect the children from anything at all. . . . She could no longer be sure they wore their seat belts, put on life jackets if they went sailing. She was virtually powerless; she could not keep them from harm. And all her efforts at having done so—"Be home after dark! Don't talk on the phone during a thunderstorm!" would be relegated to the nostalgia of their youth.*

How shall we guide teens away from dangers but toward the appropriate challenges? How do we encourage confidence but not recklessness? When do we come out with our whole protective arsenal, and when do we lay low? With such questions uppermost in our minds, it's no surprise we live with chronic cases of low- or even high-grade anxiety.

One father confesses, "The intensity of my concern, which I had expected to lessen as my daughter matured, never really did. Today she is twenty-one and tells me she rides her bicycle through the streets of Boston every day. The traffic! The pollution! She promises me that she wears a helmet, but how can a helmet adequately protect? I would like to convince her not to ride, but I know I couldn't and shouldn't."

. . . But It's Not Impossible

"Parents suffer angst over teenage children," says Joy Dryfoos, whose research in high-risk adolescent behavior is supported by The Carnegie Foundation. "There is the notion that adolescence is so difficult. In reality, however, only a small number of teens get into serious trouble. Most will go through a number of moderately worrisome experiences. Of course, in our age of guns, random violence, and AIDS, it's hard for us to draw the line between what's worrisome and what's life threatening. Despite the age we live in, teens still need room to experiment and fail. It can be hard for parents to sit back and watch this, but it's a necessary part of a teen's development."

In this chapter, we'll observe how teenagers experience both protection and overprotection. We'll learn what goes through the minds of parents as they gear up to protect teens and let them go at the right time.

First, to better understand the new turf we're standing on, let's take a look at how a parent's overprotection can disrupt adolescent development.

Overprotection Can Be a Barrier to Separation and Individuation

Adolescence, according to Dr. Roger Granet, is the second intense phase of separation and individuation a child undergoes. The first phase occurs in early childhood, between the ages of eighteen and thirty-six months. This is when the child sees herself as both a separate entity and distinctly separate from her primary caretaker; it is when the child experiences herself as an individual, a self, an autonomous person. This is not a sudden process. You might recall when your young child used to wander away from you when you were busy in the kitchen and get absorbed by blocks in the family room, only to come back to you every once in a while, to grab your leg or to ask for some juice and crackers. These little visits back were all forms of reconnecting with you, getting emotional refueling for the next bout of toddling off and being autonomous. "I am still here for you," says a parent simply by being present, reassuring the child by interacting and meeting her needs, "and when you go off again, you will know even more deeply that I am still here for you."

The second phase of separation and individuation, like the first, is a process of moving forward that contains a lot of steps backward. (It is not coincidental that many parents of teenagers will say, "I feel like I have a two-year-old in the house again!") One minute, a teenager is begging for independence, and the next, he's setting himself up to be rescued. He'll complain you don't trust him and you treat him like a baby and then, before you can turn around, he is truly acting like a two-year-old, whining and climbing into your lap. This behavior extends into the college years. I can't count how many second-semester college seniors I've taught who just can't bring themselves to finish the single "Incomplete" that keeps them from graduating and entering the "real world."

As adolescents revisit that earlier infant phase of separation-individuation, they get a second chance to work through the unfinished business that lay in their paths toward becoming separate selves.

Sending Double Messages

As this stage occurs, Dr. Granet says, overprotective parents may, on the surface, seem to be encouraging their children in their pursuit of separateness and individuation, but, in reality, they are giving their children double messages about autonomy. "Sure, you can be independent from me" is the overt message, but, as you'll see in the following conversations, a second, covert message lets a teenager know he is being released with great reluctance. What masquerades as protection and concern is, in fact, overprotection.

> "Dad, can I sleep over at Danny's?"
> "Okay . . . but by the way, don't you have a game to-

morrow? I'm not sure you'll get a good night's rest at Danny's."

Or: *"If you need me to come get you, if something goes wrong, I'll be here."*

If we want to release our teen but have some concerns that make us reluctant, we'd do better to be up front about our concerns and either suggest precautions that can be taken or, better yet, encourage our teen to devise those precautions him- or herself. For instance, if you are really worried that your son's ball game will suffer if he spends Friday night at Danny's, you might suggest Saturday night as an alternative instead of putting a damper on his fun and freedom. If your child is going away for the night, and you'll be at home, he certainly knows how to reach you by phone if he needs you. We need to listen to these kinds of "farewells" and double-check to see if they encode and communicate the thought "You're too inept to take care of yourself without me."

A Teen's Experience of Overprotection

Teens know when they're being overprotected, and they know that it injures them. Teddy, a college freshman, complains that his parents worry about everything: their parent-child relationship, his self-image, his ability to get along with teachers and other kids, mistakes he might be making. Teddy's parents may think he understands their constant worry as a form of support, but he reads it as criticism. "They always assume I'm not independent enough to be trusted. It hurts me when they treat me like something breakable and precious. What my parents are doing to me is selfish: I think they want to feel needed, so they make themselves into my big protectors. It doesn't help me to become a full human being." Teddy knows how little confidence he has, how truly difficult it is for him to make a decision. He says he would like to fashion himself into a more independent person, but he hardly knows where to start.

As you may recall from your own childhood, teens are humiliated by anything that singles them out from their friends, and being overprotected tops the list! At the Wesleyan University graduation ceremonies, I watched a father lunge toward a graduate in her cap and gown as she marched with her classmates in the procession. "Here, eat a muffin!" he commanded her. "You had no breakfast! You have low blood sugar! You're going to be sitting in the hot sun and you'll faint."

"Jesus Christ, Dad!" she said as she turned her head swiftly away from him and his muffin, uncertain which was worse—to be humiliated in front of her classmates in this way or to feel that she had no choice but to be rude to her father, who, in theory, was there that day to witness her rite of passage from student to adult.

For a teenager or young adult, overprotection is more than a matter of momentary unpleasantness. In a study of 150 undergraduates, psychologists found that the young people who believed they had been overprotected by their parents suffered greater depressive symptoms. Social anxiety, obesity, agoraphobia, panic disorders, even postpartum depression—all these problems that emerge in adulthood have been associated with overprotection.

A Hard Job Made Even Harder

Teens challenge us with their inscrutability. From the meager signs and hints they offer, it can be hard to discern precisely—or to know at all—what's going on in their lives and how they're feeling. If we're prone to worry, falling out of touch with our teen's life can put us on high alert: If we don't know what's going on, how are we supposed to protect appropriately?

Savas worries about his sixteen-year-old son, Telly. At least his nineteen-year-old, Christina, would let him know when something was going wrong. Telly, on the other hand, is self-sufficient, introverted, and rarely communicates. And the less Telly communicates, the more anxious Savas gets because he can't be there to guide him. Clueless as to what's up, Savas tends to leap to the conclusion that Telly's life is "going down the tubes."

If it's any consolation, teens notice how hard it is for parents to achieve the proper balance between protection and letting go, and they occasionally give us credit for our well-intentioned protective bungles and forgive us. While sixteen-year-old Toby may complain, "My overprotective parents stifle me in a mistaken attempt to shield me from what they perceive to be the dangers the world holds," he does admit, "When my parents overprotect, I do know that it is out of love." Carter, a college sophomore, compassionately compares his parents to others in terms of their worry and degree of flexibility: "While my parents worry about me more than most parents I know, particularly when it comes to drugs, at least they are fair with me and understand that even though they are worried, they still have to let go sometimes."

Young people are very aware that the confidence and encouragement their parents give them make a difference in their capacity to face challenges. Sally Potter, a British film director, notes that her grandmother's encouragement was crucial in her artistic development. "She always said, 'You can do whatever you set your mind to do.' She was an extremely empowering presence in my life.'"

Teens have noted that most parents get their anxieties better under control with each successive child. "My brother, who is married now, is the oldest," says fifteen-year-old Jorge, "so the parents worried every time he did something new. They were always warning him about hazards and wouldn't let him drive alone. They lightened up and became more lenient when my older sister, who's twenty-one now, wanted to do the same things. Now, when I ask to do something new, they don't worry at all because it's not new to them. Maybe they've seen that the dangers out there aren't as bad as they initially thought. I feel as if I have different parents than my older siblings; as soon as I get my permit, I know they'll let me drive."

It can happen, however, that the "baby" of a large family is often more overprotected than any of the older siblings, and teens notice this as well. Nineteen-year-old Nora explains: "I'm the last child of five, the baby. I'm the one who's always here, spending time with the parents. They've always babied me more than the others; that means they never trust me enough. For my part, I depend on them too much—I just can't break away. I want to be with my parents. If I left home, I'd miss them and they'd miss me. I tried to go away to school once, but I felt so lost and I fell apart. Now, I never do things for myself: My mom makes all my appointments, my dad fixes my car and gets it inspected. I haven't found myself. A part of me doesn't want to become an adult, have a job, do taxes."

Sometimes it's not the "literal" baby who's overprotected, but a child who is believed to be more vulnerable. Michael, a young man from New Haven, observed that his sister Sheila, the youngest sister in his family, a year older than he is, became radically sheltered in her teenage years. "My mother wanted to protect this one daughter from the world. Sheila is smart and good looking, but from the way she's been treated, you might think she's retarded or emotionally disturbed. By overprotecting Sheila, my mother is probably responding to the historical situation of black women. She fears rape, she fears anything can happen if you are poor, if you work for white people. Just now, Sheila is beginning to rebel."

Who Knows Best?

If we can penetrate a teen's inscrutability, we'll observe that they are often good judges of how much protection they need and when they're ready for an increase in independence. Still, we can't assume they're the best judges of how much or how little protection they need at the moment. However much they might protest against any restrictions, they usually do want limits, and they might only register their gratitude years later. Michael, whom you just met, reports that only now as an adult, when he looks back on his teen years, does he realize and admit that his parents "protected [his] sense of wholeness."

As a teenager, however, Michael angrily resented the extent of his parents' worry and control. The youngest of seven, he complained that while the others could return home late at night, he couldn't stay out after dark. As soon as the sun went down, he had to be inside. At fifteen, he was to be in bed by nine o'clock.

"My parents, who came from a small town, believed the city they moved to was an evil place and didn't have confidence we could make it. They feared people would take advantage of us; if we ran around with the wrong crowd, we'd get in trouble. So they protected me from the outside world."

If as a teenager, Michael found his parents' level of protection stifling, he now realizes his parents were protecting his self-esteem. He believes they succeeded. "From my family and my church community as well, I had a lot of people who were looking out for me, who loved me. Their sheltering made me believe in myself. It was only after I left my parents' protection and the protection of my community that I realized what happens to a black male in this society. I never internalized the images that the news gives of people like me. I never knew the jails were populated by people who looked like me. One Sunday, when I was going to college, I went to a suburban church with a classmate. The church elders came up to me after the service and shook my hand. They told me, 'We have black churches in the inner city.' I was so naive at the time—I thanked them for their information. It was only later that I understood they were telling me I was not welcome among them. This is what my parents were trying to protect me from."

What's Overprotection and What's Not?

First, let's distinguish overprotection from the *measured degree of worry* teens experience as loving concern. Teens are comforted when they know their parents worry about them somewhat, provided they trust that the worry is connected to real dangers and provided they believe it will let up once they're older and have proven they're trustworthy. Fourteen-year-old Randy explains that his parents are generally preparing him for greater independence. Once, however, he says, "I thought they were overprotecting me when I kept pleading to sleep over at an older friend's house and they kept refusing to let me go because they were convinced he was into drugs. They had no proof—they said they just had a bad feeling from the way he dressed and talked. I was really angry: What did they know? Everyone dressed and talked like that. I felt they should have trusted my judgment. A few months later, my friend was sent to a program for substance abusers; I didn't see it coming. That's made me take a different attitude towards my parents' judgment."

Teens are *not* comforted by worries that seem tied to their competence—or lack of it. When parents worry that their teen just won't pull through because he's inept, how can a teen respond? Either he has to accept that he's as inept as his parents think, or he has to rebel against them, filled with anger that they have underestimated his skills, his decision-making ability, and his overall maturity.

What we need to aim for is *measured concern that's in touch with our child's reality* (as opposed to "Well, when I was your age, no one in her right mind would have ever [fill in the blank]"). Alexis, an eighth grader, tells us, "My mom and dad worry about my safety and well-being, as all parents do, but they don't go to extremes. I'm allowed to go to the mall with friends, go to parties, and hang out. My parents trust me not to do anything stupid. They know I'll make the right decisions, and they respect what I decide, whatever the outcome. This makes me feel that I can trust myself to make the right choices. Their trust makes me feel as if I can do things. Since they've let me do lots of things, I know I *can* do them."

Protection versus Intrusion

Next, let's distinguish measured protection in touch with reality from the kind of overprotection that our teenagers experience as intrusiveness. Admittedly, teenagers will go through periods when any form of parental interest or protection reads as intrusion.

> *"Take an umbrella—it's going to rain."*
> *"You're always trying to control my life!"*

We have to be the judges of when we need to guide, advise, or intervene—and when we need to butt out. We have to remind ourselves that while we may still see our teens as our little darlings, they see themselves as serious people with lives and dreams of their own.

Dorothy, mother of fourteen-year-old Erin, feels confident she can generally prevent herself from being intrusive: "I try not to pry into Erin's relationships with her friends. When she brings kids home, I'm happy to meet them, but I stay far in the background, because I'm the mother and not one of the friends. I also try not to get involved in Erin's day-to-day social interactions. Erin tells me about parents who need to know every detail about their kids' love lives: They'll ask, 'Who did you dance with at the party?' I don't want to hear these things. It's not that I'm not curious and dying to know, but Erin has a right to her own privacy. After a party, I'll ask, 'Did you have a good time,' and if Erin says, 'Yeah' or 'Yuck,' I leave it at that. Erin knows that if she needs to talk to me, I'm here for her."

Protecting Our Teens, Not Ourselves

As our teens move toward competence, it helps if we keep tabs on how our own fear and reluctance can threaten to stand in their way. Meet Meg and Stuart, who know they need to put their son's emotional growth ahead of their own anxieties, but they're not having an easy time of it.

With their hearts in their throats, Meg and Stuart decided they had to permit their thirteen-year-old son, Ryan, to spend his first summer at sleep-over camp. It seemed so important to him. But they had misgivings, which they felt were reasonable. Ryan, a spacey kid, can be so deep in thought that he'll be oblivious to danger; he's the kid with his head in the clouds—the kid who would read H. G. Wells while riding his bicycle and crash into a stop sign. Ryan pays little attention to his environment, and no amount of drilling seems to help. "This," Meg explains, "has always made me sick to my stomach. We're terrified by his personality. We can't be watching him all the time. His little brother, Marty, has a totally different temperament: He's in touch with what's going on, he's in control, orderly, dependable. If you tell Marty something once, he listens. With Marty, we've hardly worried at all." This turns out to be a typical pattern: Parents of two children often state that one child (usually the older one) is more prone to risk and must be more closely protected, while the other child (usually the younger one) has an innate toughness, self-assuredness, and caution that make him or her less vulnerable.

Before Ryan left for camp, Meg and Stuart worried that no college-age camp counselor with many responsibilities and distractions of his own could keep the "otherworldly" Ryan from danger. Even the lower-risk issues agitated Meg: "Who was going to remind him to wash his face, take his vitamins, wear sunscreen?" as the summer neared, Meg and Stuart were tempted to go back on their decision, but they knew they couldn't; they had to show Ryan they recognized he was emerging as a young man. If they didn't let him go, how would he ever develop any instincts for self-protection?

Meg remembers the day he left: "His quivering independence, our cheery smiles—they were brave fronts we put up for each other. I cried all the way home."

Three weeks went by without a glitch and Meg and Stuart were beginning to wonder how they could have worried so. On visiting day, Ryan, who is enchanted by dragonflies, brought his parents down to the lake to show them where he had been making his sightings. He boasted that many mornings, unbeknownst to his counselor, he'd sneak out of his cabin before anyone was awake and swim to the other side of the lake to observe dragonflies. "I was furious," said Stuart. "How could he have been so senseless? He's not even a good swimmer! He could have slipped on slimy rocks, floated away, and no one would have even known where to look."

"All I can say," says Meg, "is that some divine providence must have been watching over him. We stood at the lake yelling, 'Do you know how dangerous it was to go out there all alone!' At least he understood why we were so upset, how parents would feel if they lost a child. Ryan was really shaken. He was crying. We were all crying. He was scared to realize that he had it in himself to do something so stupid. He kept explaining that he had been so excited by the dragonflies that he just didn't think. He didn't think! That terrifies me. He's promised never to do it anything like this again, but who knows?"

Stuart had hoped Ryan wouldn't want to go back to camp next year, but already he's asked to return and Stuart acknowledges, "We can't hold him back. He loved camp. Aside from the lake episode, Ryan handled himself, he flourished."

If we do act on our impulses to childproof a teen's world, if we think that's what we're supposed to do, we may be hit in the face with undreamed-of consequences. Marcia Ann Hain, author of a privately printed journal she kept of her son's treatment for substance abuse at Daytop Village Association, writes that as her children were growing up, she flushed away dead goldfish and replaced them without the children noticing (or so she thought)—anything to protect her children from coping with difficult, unpleasant realities, anything to childproof their world. Later, when her son was in treatment, her daughter wrote to her.

> We children always knew what you were doing with our goldfish, but were just as afraid of confronting you as you were with dealing with the issue of death with us. We were all involved in the conspiracy that made everything happy and safe. . . . Unfortunately, it wasn't always as easy to make things OK again as it was to replace a dead goldfish. Maybe that is why Andy turned to drugs . . . so at least he didn't have to feel the pain of not being able to make everything right.

Keeping Your Fears—and the Fears You Inherited—in Check

Often, if we understand the roots of our own fears, we can keep ourselves from imposing those fears on our teenagers and restricting them unnecessarily or making them unnecessarily fearful. Sometimes the fears we transmit are not even drawn from our own firsthand experience. They can be fears we've inherited from our own parents. Dorothy, fourteen-year-old Erin's mother, had to look as far back as her own mother's childhood in order to find the roots of her fear. Only then could she allow her own daughter to "have a life."

During the Depression, Dorothy's mother's parents ran a boardinghouse at the beach during the summer months. "My mother," says Dorothy, "developed a great mistrust of strangers. There were always weird people in her house, people wanted by the police. My mother feared that the boarders would do terrible things to her, yet because the family needed the money to sustain them through the winter, there was no choice but to welcome whatever strangers came their way. My mother passed her fear on to me: I'm afraid of strangers. I'm always asking, 'Who are these people?' "

One evening Erin needed to stay after school for a volleyball game, and neither Dorothy nor her husband could pick her up. She suggested Erin spend the night at one of her close girlfriend's house. But Dorothy didn't know the particular girl Erin picked and was about to complain ("Why did you have to pick a friend I don't know? Why couldn't you pick someone whose parents I know? What if they're drunken drivers, child molesters?").

If Dorothy hadn't stopped herself and told Erin she needed some time to think about the plan, surely she and Erin would have gotten into one of those "You're ruining my life, but I'm doing this for your own good" fights. By taking the time to reflect, Dorothy recognized that in this protective situation, she was experiencing her mother's fear of strangers. Through the lens of that fear, she saw Erin's situation as dangerous when it was not. Though Dorothy now recognized the source of her fear, it still blocked her from letting Erin go.

Dorothy's husband, Clifford, suggested she might calm her fears by gaining more information: "Why don't you call up this new friend's parents and introduce yourself? Say who you are and tell them you appreciate that they're taking care of Erin. Get a feel for who they are." Dorothy wasn't so sure this would help. "After all," she said, "what can you learn about people from a brief phone call? Can you say 'Hi, do you drink or abuse children' and expect to get a straight answer?"

Dorothy did call, and she had to admit the parents sounded like everyday, normal people who were as concerned about their daughter as she was about Erin. Calling reassured Dorothy, distracted her from her fears, and let her give Erin the green light for freedom. "I knew she wasn't going off to the strangers, the boardinghouse strangers."

Because Dorothy was aware that she could easily be influenced by her inherited fear, she was willing to let Clifford intervene and guide her onto a healthier path. Dorothy knows inherited fear can lead her to be more protective, more involved, more regimented than necessary. By now she knows that seeking more information can help her deal with the protective situations that are challenging or difficult. "Recognizing my fear and doing something about it is sane. I try to teach this lesson to Erin: I tell her, 'Don't get caught up in your worries. Think about the situation, do something about it if you can, and move on.'"

Driving

Teens are aware that driving is an enormous source of anxiety for any parent. Eighth-grader Alexis says, "When it comes to riding in a car with a teenage driver, my dad goes crazy, I get angry, and we have big disagreements. He forbids it, which I think is unfair, and it embarrasses me when the other kids are allowed to get rides home from a game with older friends, and I'm this dweeb who has to call home to get picked up by Daddy. I wish my dad could trust me here: I know who's a responsible driver and who's not. He knows as well as I do that there's a risk whenever you get into a car, no matter who's driving."

Many continue to be fearful about driving even when children are grown and have families of their own. "It is," says John, whose son and daughter are grown, "the most haunting of fears. When my son, Mark, visits and goes out for the evening, I'm so paranoid I can't fall asleep until I hear the garage door close. That this is illogical makes no difference. Obviously when he is in his own home in Virginia, I have no idea when he comes home. When my daughter, Renata, and her husband go on a trip, I always fight the urge to call up to hear whether they got home all right."

In my interviews, I noted that if mothers more often expressed anxiety about health and relationships, fathers were more often anxious about cars and driving. Jan, a mother of children who are nineteen and twenty explains: "I worry about who will hurt and disappoint my children, who will break their hearts. My husband dwells on the car—Is it safe enough? Is the route safe? Will the children know not to fight over a carjacking? He's always quizzing the children to be sure that everything is in tip-top shape: Did you have the oil checked? How about the brake lining? He bought them membership in the AAA, so if they break down, at least they'll be okay."

Obviously, a car poses multiple objective dangers, and many of those dangers can't be anticipated. Our child can be the safest driver and the car she drives can be well maintained and strong, but if a drunken driver runs a red light or a tractor-trailer overturns, there's no protection. For many parents, a car stands as a metaphor for all random violent acts in the world about which a parent is helpless to do anything. The reality here is that once we parents (or better yet, professional driving instructors) have taught our children to drive carefully, checked out their cars, and advised them of the safest routes, we can only hope their journeys will be unremarkable. We want to make our children well aware of all the dangers of driving, but we don't want to terrify them so much that they don't have the courage to feel competent behind the wheel.

The Biggest Fears of All:
Sex, Drugs, and Alcohol

This is frightening stuff, hard to talk about. "Oh, please," we may wish, crossing our fingers and toes, "let these not become issues in our family."

Teens understand that sex, drugs, and alcohol are dangerous, but they may see themselves as invulnerable to danger. Parents who act overprotectively when it comes to sex, drugs, and alcohol typically dwell on the potential dangers and act drastically to curtail a teenager's freedom, as if that might really help. Of course, such an approach tends to backfire. If we look back at our own teen years, we'll probably recall that the more violently our parents curtailed our freedoms and the more authoritarian their stance, the more we were bent on flagrant rebellion.

Researcher Joy Dryfoos offers excellent advice to the parents of teens: "Parents need to be authoritative, not authoritarian. You need communicate openly long before problems arise. You need to keep repeating messages about safety, to assure your teen that while it's interesting to try these tempting things and everyone out there seems to be doing it, you hope she'll be able to resist." That way, when the time comes for your child to consider experimenting with drugs or sexual relations, your thoughts about safety will have already been registered in his or her mind. Your teenager will know, for instance, that you think it is difficult to protect oneself against sexually transmitted diseases and the modes of protection are not always reliable. Your child will be able to consider where you stand when he or she makes decisions regarding sex.

If we have established a trusting dialogue with our teens and continue to offer information and our opinions about sex, drugs, and alcohol, we're certainly moving in the right direction. But we all know that talk alone might not provide all the protection we are bent on providing. We can protect our teens and reassure ourselves we have done our very best by taking concrete, active steps. This might mean enrolling a teen in a youth program about the hazards of sex, drugs, and alcohol. It might mean providing religious instruction clarifying the belief that premarital sex is not acceptable. It might mean having a teen inoculated against hepatitis B or supplying the condoms. Leni, mother of two teens, says, "We have given our children a strong religious faith and an ethnic identity that will hopefully sustain them as they encounter things on their own. We're always preaching what we believe. We raise questions. I sit the kids down if there's a TV show on drugs or AIDS and make them watch it together with me. I want them to see what happens to kids who experiment with drugs, who are loose in their sexual behavior. They say, 'Oh, Mom, we know all that. Do you think we'd do those things?' I say, 'Still, I want you to listen.'"

Parents Negotiating

What happens when parents don't agree about how much protection a teenager or young adult needs? What if one parent thinks intrusion is called for and the other believes it is better to lie low or butt out altogether? Usually parents who hold different protective strategies are able to compromise, acting as checks and balances for each other. But during the teen years, when a child's success and happiness in "real life" seems to be at stake, reaching a compromise becomes more challenging and sometimes just isn't possible.

When parents take distinctly different stances toward protection and fail to negotiate a compromise, it is still useful for them to continue articulating each of their positions. Savas, the father we have met earlier, is worried that his son, Telly, is not doing as well in school as he used to. Leni, the mother, says they should be counting their blessings. "When my husband sees a C on Telly's report card, he thinks Telly is throwing his life away. There's a lot worse that can go wrong for a teen besides a few C's on a report card."

But Savas has high expectations for his son and feels Telly is letting his mother and father down and, more important, letting himself down. Leni is furious that Savas would judge a child on the basis of his performance in school the same way he might judge his employees on the basis of their productivity.

Telly will be applying for college in two years. Savas feels it is his parental obligation to protect his son from ruining his chances. "Standards are standards," Savas insists.

"Not when you're raising a teen," says Leni. "It's we who can't deal with the thought that Telly might not handle school as well as he used to." As she sees it, Telly is coming into his own: He's deciding what his goals are, what's important to him. Just as adults might behave strangely if they're having a midlife crisis and thinking "Hey, is this all there is to life?" so might teenagers. "Telly is a good kid!" says Leni. "He doesn't drink or hang out at all hours with the wrong crowd. There are other standards we've held the children to, and here Telly more than measures up."

Both Leni and Savas have valid points of view. After battling this issue through, neither has convinced the other that he or she is more on target. While a younger child does better if his parents can present a unified protective approach, a teenager can accept that his parents have different heartfelt opinions that need to be expressed and considered. As for Telly, he can be guided well by both his parents' messages: His mother will assure him that he is a good kid, regardless of how he does at school, and his father will help him to see why doing well in school now will be to his advantage later.

Limiting the Blame

A warning here: There will be times when, despite our best intentions, we fail to anticipate and protect our teens against all the dangers they might encounter. We'll blame ourselves, perhaps vowing to be more restrictive next time; but that's unfair to ourselves and unfair to our teens.

When our children were small, if we neglected to pack an extra, dry set of clothing for nursery school, we might have had reason to blame ourselves for not anticipating that our kind-of-toilet-trained child might need a change of clothes. If we didn't insist that our child wear the bicycle helmet just to ride to a friend's and he took a spill, sure, we'd have reason to kick ourselves for not insisting. We should have known better—we should have anticipated the dangers and the consequences. *But in the teenage years, the relative dangers of a protective situation can often be evaluated only after it's all played out.*

Consider Victoria's story. What happened to her son, in fact, was far from the worst thing that could happen to a teenager—but she won't forgive herself, thinking that if only she had been more scrupulous, she might have protected him differently.

At first Victoria had been so pleased. Kenneth, her shy, reclusive sixteen-year-old who spends most of his time in his room conversing anonymously on the Internet, had agreed to go to a school dance with a date. Maybe this meant he was finally coming out of his shell. He said he knew what kids wore to the school dances (jeans and good shirts and ties), but just to be sure, knowing Kenneth might be out of touch, Victoria decided to go the extra mile and checked out the dress policy with a colleague who had a son in another high school, and it seemed right. She took Kenneth to the mall and helped him pick out a black shirt, a red silk tie, and new jeans. Everything, Victoria thought, was set. For sure she had done her part.

On the night of the dance, she dropped Kenneth off at school, where he would meet his date. Victoria wanted to peek in, curious to see if everything was working out, but she felt Kenneth needed his privacy at this juncture, so, continuing to do what she believed was the right thing, she drove off.

Apparently when Kenneth attempted to enter the building, an adult who had been hired to monitor the dance told him that he needed to be wearing a suit, not jeans, and would not be allowed to enter until he went home and changed. Too humiliated to tell the monitor that he needed to get into the building to call home, Kenneth walked to the only phone booth he knew, one near a diner three blocks away from the school. When he told his mother his predicament, he neglected to mention that he was waiting at the diner. As Victoria drove round and round the school, growing more and more frantic, Kenneth gave up waiting and walked home through a deserted business area that was considered unsafe at night. When he finally came home, he couldn't be persuaded to go back to the dance, even to let his date know he wouldn't be there. There was a big crying and yelling scene.

That night, Victoria lay in bed chastising herself for each protective decision she felt she had bungled, even though at the time her choices had seemed so right. Why hadn't she checked out the dress code with a parent who had a child in the same school? Why hadn't she stuck around the school long enough to see that her son was safely inside? Why had she assumed she would pick her son up in front of school? Why had she assumed her son would know that he was never to walk through the business district at night, no matter what?

Monday morning, Victoria chewed the school out for their irresponsibility—for humiliating her son, for putting him at physical risk. But that hasn't changed the damage to her son. "Since then," Victoria worries, "he hasn't gone out to socialize. He goes to school, he comes back to the computer." Victoria continues to worry about the school dance episode, and it's herself she berates: "I think about what could have happened to him that night in the business district. People get shot there all the time. I think about the long-term emotional damage this could have." Each night, as she lay in bed, she always prays that Kenneth will be safe. Then something like this happens, and she asks herself, "What more could I have done?"

Probably nothing. Unless parents of teens have crystal balls, we won't always get it right, because there are too many variables that are beyond anticipation. It's a fact, and we can only do our best to come to terms with it: We simply don't have ultimate control.

Young People with Special Needs

Young people with special physical or emotional challenges may require special or ingenious modes of protection. But that protection needs to be given in measured doses that are adequate, appropriate, and respectful of the young person's need for autonomy. It's no surprise that in a study of adolescents with chronic disabilities, a parent's overprotection was determined to lower self-esteem and increase anxiety.

I want to return again to Sophia, the wise and courageous mother whom you met earlier. At every step along the way, Sophia was sorely tempted to overprotect her physically handicapped son, Jed, when he became a young adult. By making Jed's need for independence her priority, she has been able to keep her overprotective impulses in check.

An overarching thought has guided Sophia: "Jed must feel adequate to make his own judgments. How could I give him the confidence to make his own judgments if I kept telling him, 'This is going to happen to you!' 'Do this or you'll get sick!' A child slowly begins to internalize your distrust, begins to feel inadequate about himself and his ability to make decisions and handle some reasonable risk. Risk has to be weighed. We're always handling some risk, and we make mistakes, but mistakes are what we learn from. If you go through life thinking that a tragedy is going to occur, you might as well lock yourself up in the bathroom, because tragedies can happen. The hardest thing in the world, for me, is not to make my child afraid. If he's afraid of life, then he doesn't live. That's a handicap."

Sophia knows she can't worry about Jed's happiness; this he must assure for himself. "No one is happy all the time or sad all the time. For me to want Jed to be happy all the time is stupid, unrealistic, and puts unrealistic pressure on him."

At seventeen, Jed said he wanted to go backpacking with a

friend in Europe. "Backpacking?" Sophia asked. "Like hitch-hiking and walking up mountains?"

"Yeah," he said. "I really want to do that."

Sophia's gut reaction was to say, "You can't do that! What if no one picks you up and you're walking for miles?" But she told Jed, "If that's what you want to do, terrific." He went backpacking in Ireland and England. He was gone for months and had a wonderful time. "Of course," says Sophia, "I'd get these calls in the middle of the night: 'Mom, I've got terrible news for you! I fell and broke both my artificial legs.' I was pretty hysterical at first, but this would happen again and again over the years. Jed would locate a prosthetic maker, and quite literally, someone would carry him there. Having dealt with this kind of stuff, you can understand why I never got too anxiety-ridden about Jed going out without a sweater."

Some Signs You May Be Overprotecting a Teenager

Your Child

- ❑ turns to you to make decisions she can make for herself;
- ❑ has many fears that restrict where she is willing to go and what challenges she might take on;
- ❑ perceives himself as fragile or bound to fail;
- ❑ has little self-confidence;
- ❑ consistently complains that you are intrusive and offer no privacy;
- ❑ lies frequently in order to participate in activities most other peers are permitted to do;
- ❑ prefers staying home alone to participating in activities with friends.

You

- ❑ cause your child to question her ability to accomplish what she sets out to do;

❑ encourage your child to be dependent on you by doing things for him that he can do for himself;

❑ give your child the feeling that he is endangered and in need of your protection;

❑ discourage your child from striving and taking risks when she is uncertain and fearful;

❑ teach your child that no one can be trusted outside the immediate family;

❑ treat your child in a babyish way;

❑ discourage your child from taking on age-appropriate responsibilities;

❑ hide sad, disturbing, or unpleasant news.

Things You Can Do to Let Go of Teens

❑ When appropriate, let them make decisions for themselves and experience the positive and negative consequences of their decisions.

❑ As long as a new situation isn't life-threatening, give them a shot at experiencing it so they can overcome their fears. Having equipped them with the skills and precautionary measures, offer your wholehearted blessings.

❑ Listen to what they are saying. Support them in their efforts to discover who they are and who they might be. Trust you will discover they are even more capable than you think.

❑ Remind yourself how violently you resented parental intrusion when you were a teen. Try to empathize with what teens might be feeling.

❑ Wait for teens to express a need for comfort before you offer it.

❑ Realize you can't always be there to correct mistakes and push aside the bullies. Allow teens to fend for themselves when appropriate.

❏ Search for ways to stay calm and reduce your own anxiety. Johann, a father of grown children, recalls that he accomplished this "by spending a great deal of time training children to be attentive to safety when they were younger. We taught them that they were responsible for their own safety and that the older children were responsible for the younger ones. While we never limited their activities, because we didn't want them to be fearful, we always discussed potential dangers with them, and since they were adventurous, such discussions were frequent! From early on, I always taught my children to be self-sufficient, and I believe that has helped them shape their lives. I tried to make the children feel that I consider them to be responsible people. Today, one of my greatest satisfactions as a father is to hear my adult children say, 'You have always treated us as equals.' "

❏ Let teens make their own mistakes. Barbara, a dean of admissions and mother of two children, explains: "Mistakes are what we learn from. Being a parent is about having anxiety and not letting it govern you. Naturally I want my children to be safe and happy all the time, but that's not going to happen. They're going to be living with happiness and sadness, comfort and pain. To want them to be safe and happy all the time is unrealistic. It's an enormous pressure on them and it would make me crazy. By now, I have to trust that my children are reasonably good managers of their lives. I dispense advice, but just as often, my kids dish out advice to me. I've always believed overly cautious parents create anxious kids, and I've seen it played out among my kids' peers who have grown into nervous wrecks or timid mice like their parents. Overly cautious parents rob kids of joy. A child who's not allowed to experiment has a narrow life. When my kids consider challenges they may face, I don't ask them why I ask them why not. As we get older, life inevitably closes down on us, narrowing our horizons. I want to encourage my children to keep their horizons broad and wide open for as long as they can."

f You Have a Teen, These Are Some of the More Common Protective Decisions You're Likely to Be Making

Being Alone

❑ If your child is sick, can he stay home alone while you are at work?

❑ Can your child stay home alone if you will be away overnight?

Traveling

❑ Can your child drive or take a bus or train alone or with friends?

❑ Can your child visit older friends in college?

❑ Can your child go camping with friends without adult supervision?

Social Life

❑ Will you allow your child to date whomever he chooses; go to the parties of his choice; pick the friends and crowd he chooses to go around with?

❑ Will you interfere if your child insists he would rather be alone most of the time?

❑ Can your child go to unchaperoned parties or be alone in a house with a boyfriend or girlfriend?

❑ Will you permit your child to go steady? Become engaged?

School

❑ Can your child pick the course of study she prefers; pick the after-school activities of interest or drop ones she loses interest in; go out for football or wrestling?

❑ Can your child apply to the colleges she wishes to or join the military? How much guidance is appropriate for you to give?

Equipment and Machines

❑ Can your child drive a car alone; be driven by friends?

❑ Can your child ride a motorcycle, moped, motorboat, sailboat?

Emotional Well-Being

❑ How can you tell if your child is mildly depressed or is seriously considering suicide? When do you let the blues pass, and when do you get professional help?

❑ How can you tell if your child is just watching his weight or has a serious eating disorder?

Economics

❑ Do you encourage your child to get a job?

❑ Is your child free to spend her allowance and earnings?

❑ If your child must buy clothing out of an allowance, is she free to make independent choices?

Substance Abuse and Sex

❑ Do you prohibit cigarettes and alcohol or accept they will be used with moderation?

❑ Do you make efforts to control your child's sexual activity?

How will you react if you suspect or learn your child is sexually active?

❑ Do you assume your child knows better than to use drugs, or do you suspect it is always a possibility?

Physical Autonomy

❑ Can your child consult a doctor alone?

❑ Can your child administer her own medicines?

❑ Will you permit your child to have ears (or other body parts) pierced; get a tattoo; dye or shave hair?

❑ Will your child be permitted to have plastic surgery for cosmetic reasons?

PART
THREE

9

Protective Rituals

"With our children," theologian Michael Wyshogrod once told me, "God really has us over a barrel." This evokes Freud's most poignant description of love and loss:

> *We are never so defenseless against suffering as when we love, never so helplessly unhappy as when we have lost our loved object or its love.*

You may think we have considered just about everything we can possibly do to protect children wisely and keep our own anxieties under control. One area remains: protective rituals, a most potent resource that parents of all cultures turn to in order to contain and channel the terror they hold for their children's physical and emotional well-being.

Rituals of protection are not meant to take the place of concrete methods of protection, such as teaching safety, being prudent, taking painstaking efforts to avoid accident, and seeking medical attention. Through the rituals, we recognize that beyond all the precautions we take for our children and insist they take for themselves, we are ultimately impotent against random evil, uncontrollable danger, and bad luck—we are unable to guarantee a child's absolute safety. The rituals permit us to ensnare courage, confidence, hope, and the illusion of control; they open the door for us to bless and then let go.

Anxious parents have been able to find solace and strength in amulets, talismans, charms, relics, shrines, blessed oils, incantations, fasts, confessions of sin, and offerings of charity in return for blessing. They have held ceremonies for birth, naming, coming of age, healing, and performed exorcisms. They have protected children with such materials as blue stones, red threads, a parent's spit, dried eyes of sacrificed sheep, ugly names, dirty clothes, green wreathes, and pictures of saints.

Fusing Concrete and Ritual Protection

In "Snake Spoke," based on a story in Chinese folklore, we learn of a father who, before allowing his son to leave home, "took a charm from around his neck and tied it around his son's neck." And the father said, "This has the name of the Protector written on it. The priest who sold it to me said it would chase any demon away. Even so, remember: hasty head, hasty feet, hasty end."

—From the story "Snake Spoke"

Some protective practices originate in official religion, some evolve from folk practices, and others synthesize official and folk practice by weaving together a little bit of this and a little bit of that. The stakes being so high, parents have always been resourceful in their ritual response to protection, improvising as they go along, feeling free to use whatever might work.

How do the protective rituals that parents perform for children work? They neither replace the literal work of protection nor substitute for seat belts, helmets, knee pads, condoms, and all of our lessons. They do provide a means of mental healing for parents. By enabling us to represent our internal struggles

Protective Rituals in Greece and Rome

In order to secure blessings for their nieces and nephews, aristocratic Roman matrons attended the festival of the Matralia and worshipped the goddess Matuta, "a female figure holding children in the security of her lap." They offered toasted cakes to the goddess in order to seek her protection.

Infants and children in ancient Greece and Rome were considered especially susceptible to the evil eye. Aunts or grandmothers would lift a baby from it cradle and apply spit to its forehead to protect it from danger. If a stranger entered a house and saw the child sleeping, a nurse would spit three times in the face of the stranger.

Parents believed loving a child too much could bring on disaster. Thus, Epictetus records the following advice in practicing restraint: "If you kiss your child . . . never allow your fancy free rein, nor your exuberant spirits to go as far as they like, but hold them back, stop them, just like those who stand behind generals when they ride in triumph, and keep reminding them that they are mortal."

In Greece, in the early 1800s, a stranger who praised his host's fine sons was made to spit in their faces to undo the evil effect of his praise. Then the mother mixed dust from the ground with oil from a lamp burning before a picture of the Virgin and put a patch of this mixture on her sons' foreheads.

and process our feelings, rituals allow us to reduce our anxiety enough to let go.

Many of the ancient protective measures, ridiculed as superstition or maligned as magic, have been abandoned, and that is a pity, for their healing powers are genuine. Most of us are aware that current medical research has demonstrated how belief, hope, prayer, courage, humor, and distraction can strengthen immunity and speed up a patient's recovery. In family life, rituals serve a similar positive function. Ritualized activities, such as having a certain way to sit, eat, and converse during a meal, or certain predictable ways to spend leisure time, celebrate birthdays, spend vacations, or react to illness, serve to transmit the values of the family from one generation to another and to promote emotional adjustment.

The performance of protective rituals gives symbolic form to our most deeply felt hopes. As we perform the ritual, we externalize what Mary Douglas, an anthropologist of ritual, called our "internal states"—naming them, getting them out in the open. When fears for our children cause us to lose our sense of control and our focus, protective rituals can heal us, concentrate our attention, comfort us, sustain us, shore us up, and bring us back to that stable, whole place from which we are able to function once again.

If the rituals we perform are also performed by our extended family or our community, we experience a unification of our private hopes with the hopes of others whose love and values we share. If we, out of alienation or lapsed interest, do not practice the protective rituals of the religious or ethnic culture we were raised in—say Christian baptism ceremonies or rituals of protection against the evil eye—we may still take comfort in knowing that such protective rituals are practiced and that the intense, overwhelming fears we experience for our children aren't ours alone.

Some parents believe that performing a protective ritual will literally keep their children safe. They have confidence in God or a divine being who hears and answers the prayers parents utter on behalf of their children. They believe that the divine presence will shield their vulnerable children.

I know this was the case for my grandfather Charles. An especially fearful parent and grandparent, my grandfather cried when his children or grandchildren left his presence to go to school, to the grocer, or to work, and he would cry out of joy and relief when they returned, always greeting them with the expression *gezunt oifn keppele*, "blessings on your head." Imagine how he might have reacted when his children and grandchildren were to travel abroad! Curiously, he could handle that, because he had a ritual solution that enabled him to protect and release.

He would give the departing child or grandchild a dollar bill (in later years, taking note of inflation—as he assumed God also did—he upped this to five dollars, and he would instruct his child or grandchild to give it to a beggar or person collecting charity upon arriving at the destination.

Here was the rationale behind his folk practice, one which is still carried out by many people today. My grandfather believed that a person who was in the process of carrying out a divine commandment would be protected by God from the time the deed was begun until the time it was completed. From the time Grandfather gave us the money, until we arrived and donated it, he believed we could be assured a safe passage.

The point isn't that my grandfather's dollar bills kept our planes from having engine troubles, but rather that performing the ritual distracted him from his terror long enough to let us go. The ritual made him feel he had done all he could do, and he knew he had done his best. He had found a way to deal with his uncertainty about our fate.

Many people do not have complete faith in the efficacy of protective rituals but perform them just the same. This is not an atypical stance people take toward ritual in general. Perhaps you've known people who have been alienated by the "hocus-pocus" of their religions, but when it comes time to plan a family funeral, they want it done "right," with an official member of the clergy reciting the conventional liturgy. It is possible to disbelieve in a ritual's power but still perform it with solemnity, hope, and expectation. This is not about hypocrisy or hedging bets; rather, I think it's about the human potential of containing belief and disbelief simultaneously.

Neither disbelief nor ambivalence need stand in the way of our performing protective rituals. A New York City merchant of amulets—hamsas, anti–evil eye rings, necklaces, and key-chains—had just finished affixing amulets, given to him as gifts from his fellow dealers, all over the crib of his newborn baby. I asked him if he really thought they would make a difference. "Some say it's superstition," he said. "Some say it's hogwash. Who knows? You hear all these stories of terrible things that happened to families that don't take precautions. But it doesn't hurt to do it, so why take a chance?" While the merchant doesn't altogether believe in the amulets, he has strong feelings about how they should be properly used. He would never buy an amulet for his own child; it has to be a present from someone else and in that way function as a sign of the family or community pulling together in hope.

A ritual shared with me by Ayala Guy, an educator whose mother came from Poland, comes to mind. "I was a very healthy baby, and I was never sick," Ayala explained. "Every day my mother took me for a stroll in the park, and there were many other mothers doing the same thing. Once in a while, a mother and baby would be missing for one, two, or three days. When she returned, everybody would ask, 'Where were you?' She'd say, 'Oh, the baby was sick and I stayed home.' This would happen to all the babies except me. I was always healthy. My mother was afraid people would say, 'Oh, Ayala is never sick.' So periodically, my mother would keep me home for a day. When she came back to the park, she'd say, 'The baby was sick, so I stayed home.' This is how she protected me from the other mothers who might be jealous of my good health and put a curse on me. When my mother told me this story, I found it so sweet. She said, 'You know, I am not really superstitious, but it doesn't hurt.' "

Theologian Neil Gilman explains the phenomenon of turning to ritual for protection in this way: "Whenever we are overwhelmed by natural events and feel powerless to control our destinies, we intuitively seek some device that we believe will enable us to regain control and bend nature to our will." Gilman uses the term *magicalist* to describe ritual that is "motivated by the belief that it has the power to effect a substantive change in the nature of things out there." Is magicalist the right term, I wonder? I do not think that people who perform such rituals, particularly those marking transitional or "liminal" states, actually believe they are changing the course of nature. They do not believe that the prayers they say or rituals they perform for their children's safety will literally work like magic. Such ceremonies serve as *metaphors* of divine protection, as Heather Murray Elkins, a professor of liturgical studies, explains: "When we baptized our son Daniel at sixteen months, the ceremony was literally meant to affirm the faith of his parents and godparents. But as I saw it, I felt that the baptism placed an indelible mark, like a tattoo, on the spirit of my child. Call it magic if you will, but I felt the mark which was a metaphor that signaled God's irresistible grace."

Why do so many parents, even those who generally don't observe religious ceremonies, turn to protective rituals at times of crisis in their children's lives? When I consider why so many Jewish parents, even those who don't see themselves as particularly religious, choose to mark the birth of a son with the ritual ceremony of circumcision—a particularly invasive ritual, to be sure—it strikes me, as I have written in the journal *Tikkun*, that:

"We get out the powerful magic of our people to usher us through the threatening thresholds. . . . I don't think we believe some hocus-pocus we perform can coerce God into giving us what we want.

"We who reach out for amulets and ceremonies that will protect and keep a newborn alive . . . are reaching for assurance. Everything we can do for our newborns seems insufficient to protect them from their fragility. It's not enough to have engaged the best obstetrician and the most respected pediatrician, or to have purchased the crib whose safety research has sanctioned. Even keeping a cribside vigil to make sure the baby is still breathing is not enough. Our powerlessness is overwhelming. By turning to ancient ritual, we turn wisely to a road map to safety. The ceremony steadies us and we regain some control."

When parents perform rituals for their children's well-being, when we pray for their protection, we acknowledge, as theologians Ann and Barry Ulanov explain, that "we know our love is not powerful enough to protect them from all harm. . . . Praying for them changes our love from a closed to an open hand, from a hand that tightly holds them under rein to one that holds them loosely. Praying for them makes us supple and flexible in our love for them."

But understand: Many parents (and I count myself in this group) who perform rituals to protect children and to extend our blessings over them in our absence, *do not* necessarily have a literal belief that these rituals of protection will act as shields for our children. We don't believe that performing the ritual itself will assure their safety or health or prevent their suffering. Nor do we believe that if we forget to perform the ritual or perform it incorrectly or without proper honor or emotional intention our children's lives will be endangered. We do not perform protective rituals assuming we have the power to influence a divine response. As author Harold Kushner has taught, many of us accept that our prayers for our children's safety, health, and happiness will not always be answered as we wish them to be, even if we and our kids are the "good people" to whom "bad things" really shouldn't happen. From Kushner we've learned that when our children experience misfortune, we shouldn't assume that God has singled them out for suffering in order to teach them or us something, like compassion and gratitude. (What compassionate God, we ask, would ever inflict fatal diseases upon children in order to teach anyone compassion?) Certainly, we shouldn't assume that the misfortunes our children experience are signs of punishment.

Those of us of fickle faith still perform rituals to protect our children, praying for their well-being. Disregarding the outcome of the protective ritual, we perform it, giving concrete expression to our fears. In performing a ritual, we face the reality of our fear and own it; we are reconciled with the fact that there are issues over which we have little control. Through the ritual, we let our children know how profoundly we care. We let them know that our protective wish follows them when they've left our presence. Generally, children do have good memories of their parents' protective rituals, even though, at the time, they may appear to be oblivious to or annoyed by them.

I asked a group of college students to describe ways in which their parents conveyed a sense of safety, and many named family rituals. "My mother would always sprinkle our rooms with holy water during thunderstorms," said Dorothy. "Interestingly enough, today I have absolutely no fear of thunderstorms." Michael recalls that his mother was deathly scared when there was thunder and lightning. "It meant that God was speaking. When there was thunder and lightening, my mother gathered us children into her prayer closet, and there she would pray. I knew I was grown up and could handle myself when I wasn't taken into the closet. I learned to pray, I always prayed as a child, and I pray now. God talks to me and gives me direction."

"All my parents had to do to give me a feeling of being safe," said Bret, "was to keep their door a little bit open and keep the hall light on. Even when I was bigger, seeing their open door in the light gave me the feeling that my protectors were near."

"Before I went to bed," said Alissa, "my parents listened to me say my prayers. When they said the word 'goodnight,' I felt safe."

Nan, a graduate student, grew up in a devout Catholic family. Today she would not think of traveling anywhere without an old Saint Christopher medal and Our Lady of the Highway in her car. "I get this from my grandmother, who is into saints and stuff. She knows the patron saint of everything. From my grandmother and parents, I know that God loves me and wouldn't let anything terrible happen to me without some kind of reason. I pray as I travel. I sing songs as I walk alone so I never feel that I'm all by myself: 'I'm Not Alone' or 'My Father Is with Me Wherever I Go.' Mostly, even though we don't discuss it, I know that my grandmother and parents are praying for me everyday and that makes a big difference."

Protective Wishes

Freud wrote that we can "assume that primitive man had great confidence in his wishes." Being modern, rational people, we do not have so much confidence in the power of our wishing. We may believe (or fear) that there is simply no logical, scientific relationship between what we wish for and what comes to pass. Yet on a level, perhaps beneath our awareness, beneath our screen of rationality, we who are parents do indeed make wishes for our children. We wish our bloody hearts out. Keep my child safe, sane, whole. Keep me preserved through my child. As we wish, we focus our attention into a pinpoint of sharp light, rearranging the universe the way poems rearrange language and make beauty, transforming words and objects, through ritual, into the symbolic conduits of our hopefulness. No, of course, the protective wishes of parents for children don't always materialize, but that does not deny the power of our wishing, the art of our longing.

Some of us perform protective rituals that have been handed down to us in our religious traditions, either as formal practices or as practices that bear the idiosyncratic stamps of our own households. Many of the home-based protective rituals are practiced and officiated over by mothers and grandmothers, as the home has been the domain of female religious expertise in many religious traditions, particularly when the rituals performed at home concern the well-being of children.

Some of us, whether we are connected or unconnected to religious traditions, practice protective rituals of our own devising, which serve the same function as official religious rituals. As theologian Tom Driver notes, "To speak of ritual is not necessarily to speak of religion." Like time-hallowed, traditional rituals, the ones we devise also allow us to name our fears for our children, offer hope that they will not be realized, and then get on with the business of carefully and appropriately letting go. These can be daily rituals, such as those we perform at bedtime or as our children go off to school, or they can be rituals performed only once for each child: that painful bit-by-bit send off on the first day of kindergarten, the long drive a father and child take up to college, complete with the current version of the "facts of life" lecture. These can be rituals that do not feel like rituals at all: Sociologists James H. S. Bossard and Eleanor S. Boll note that just because we don't exorcise demons when illness comes to our households doesn't mean we no longer have rituals surrounding illness.

> *Though people today seldom dress in a frightening costume and beat the air with sticks in order to drive out evil spirits, families have very special procedures surrounding illness. Such procedures involve not only the uses of certain medicines and medical devices, but frequently require a special room, bed, games, food and bathing techniques. . . . These rituals, though they have lost in pomp and rigidity, are called forth by the . . . anxiety and desire to do something constructive.*

In my household, we have our own rituals for sickness that represent our wishes for healing: We always tell a sick child she can spend the day in mommy and daddy's bed, and we solicitously offer the same special "sick foods"—flat soda, cut-up fruits, crushed ice ("snow") with Coca-Cola syrup, or hot Jell-O.

Even the toys we give our children can represent our protective wishes and denote our concern that our children develop a capacity for self-protection. It's no surprise that one of the hottest, most desired items of a recent Christmas season was a collection of action figures known as Mighty Morphin Power Rangers. These are action figures based on a children's television show about the Rangers, who are described as teenagers who practice gymnastics and karate in their continuous battle with four evil aliens. A parent's wish to empower a child against evil may account for the popularity of such gifts as Superman and Batman capes, plastic knight's shield and armor, and even, disregarding the violence they appear to endorse, guns and swords. If you've ever seen a child who wears his Superman cape day and night and observed his parent rarely urging him to take it off, you will have seen a toy—or, specifically, a child's costume—functioning as a kind of amulet. The books and films we hope our children will find endearing often contain spells, devices, or characters whose role is to enable self-protection or to provide guardianship: Note the popularity of Dorothy's ruby slippers, Luke Skywalker's "May the Force be with you," and Peter Pan's Tinkerbell.

One mother has deep fears about her child riding off on her bike to visit a friend down the street. But the child is nine, a competent rider, and the street is safe and quiet. Each and every time before her child goes off, there is a prescribed litany. The mother says, "Remember to take your helmet." The child answers, "I never forget my helmet." "Don't just take it, put it on," says the mother. "Okay, okay," says the child. "I want you to call me when you get there," says the mother. "Do I have to?" "Yes!" "Give me a kiss. Good-bye!" "Good-bye!" the litany ends, and as the exchange is sealed with the intimate gesture of the kiss, we're reminded that the word *good-bye*, the word we nearly always utter as our children leave our presence, is a contraction of the words "God be with you." This conversation is not about safety instruction alone, while that is a crucial component. It is not just about the polite way to leave someone's presence, while etiquette, too, plays a part. This is a ceremony, a ritual of departure to help bridge the transition between being safe and watched at home and being safe and watching out for oneself in the world. With faith that she has equipped her child with knowledge and blessing, with faith the child will return, this mother can let her go.

What Leads Us to a Ritual Response

We can experience fears for our children that are so intense that we are rendered unable to carry on our work of sustaining life. Fear can serve a useful function for parents: It awakens us, warns us, goads us to action. But fear can also cripple, rendering us panic-stricken and immobile. Fear can cause us to lose our own "shield"—that mechanism that allows us to limit our awareness of possible disasters sufficiently so that we are able to carry on. By performing a protective ritual, we acknowledge that fear impairs our ability to function. Through the ritual, we acknowledge the loss of our shield against fear and attempt to restore it. While some protective rituals do take place in houses of worship or are officiated over by clergy (such as baptisms or circumcision ceremonies) for the most part, protective rituals are performed at home, and it is the parent who takes on the role of ritual expert and in doing so reflects his or her personal style and cultural heritage. The parent will orchestrate the ritual, determining its pace, duration, the props, symbols, language, sounds and smells, gestures, and who participates and who witnesses.

Protective rituals connect to life crises of all different magnitudes that our children encounter. Some life crises occur daily, such as the crisis of leaving the physical and emotional safety of home and family and venturing into the outer world. Other life crises just crop up, such as the crisis of sickness, of going off on a trip or adventure, of having a critical exam to take (one woman I know used to telephone her friends and asked them to say a prayer for her son at the exact time he'd be taking an exam. He made it—or at least his mom made it!—through high school, college, and medical school.)

Here, then, are some of the rituals performed by our contemporaries. My hope is that they will inspire you to recognize and value your own rituals of protection and letting go, and to create new ones.

Contemporary Rituals of Protection

Protection for Newborns

Anne Carson, author of *Spiritual Parenting in the New Age*, was aware that when parents of all cultures note the fragility of their newborns, "There exists an instinctual desire to put some kind of stamp, a copyright or registration on the child. And so we have birth certificates, baptisms, circumcision rites, and special baby scrapbooks, all to imprint the child's existence onto the world, to enroll him or her in the Book of Life."

When her own child was born, Carson began her own protections by choosing a traditional name, Catherine, instead of one she originally liked, Cerridwen, the name of the Welsh goddess of the cauldron. Why the switch? She did not "want to attract the attention of the gods, to tempt the hand of fate." Carson marked the baby's birth with a "rite of paganing—a ritual dedication of our baby to the forces of earth, water, sun and sky." This ceremony, which took place outdoors, with friends and family standing in a circle, begins as the father picks up the baby and presents her to the sky. He asks that the child be blessed, protected, and granted "wisdom, inspiration, and wonder." He passes the baby to the mother, who asks the "Earth, Mother of all," to bless the child with eternal strength, a seeking spirit, and a sense of rootedness.

Telephoning

"We worry about our children and grandchildren every minute of the day," says Cherie, a South Carolina nurse who has eight grown children and twelve grandchildren. Being Baptists, Cherie and her husband, James senior, protected every child and grandchild through the ritual of baptism. "Jesus Christ was baptized," says James senior, "so I believe he's protecting the children completely when they're baptized."

But for more daily, and less cosmic, protection, Cherie and James senior channel their fears and worries by regularly calling the children. "When we telephone," says Cherie, "we're always telling them how they should protect themselves and their own children. We don't worry if we drone on." You'll note that repeating important information and warnings over and over again, until the parent has no doubt that the child is saturated, is also a ritualized aspect of Cherie and James senior's protective strategy. Regularity and anticipation also play a part: Each child knows when to expect his or her weekly phone call, and so the call itself—making it, receiving it (let alone the contents of the communication)—has taken on a ritual function for both the parents and the child.

Daily Prayer

Daily prayer is a major part of this family's regular regimen. "We pray for the children all the time, morning, noon and night," says Cherie. "Just as we maintain phone conversation with the children, we maintain a prayer conversation with God. My prayers go from my heart to Jesus. From Jesus, the prayers go out to the children. I pray that each child has a good life and nothing ever happens to them. Sometimes I'll say the twenty-third Psalm, you know, 'The Lord is my shepherd, I shall not want.' But usually I use my own words: 'Protect them as they're going, protect them as they're coming.' "

Each summer, when Cherie and James hold their family reunion, they pray together for protection. Before their meal, all two hundred relatives will sit at two long tables and hold hands, making a living chain. Every child and grandchild must find a place in the chain and hold on, too, so they're well woven in. Together they say, "Dear God, Protect our coming and protect our going and bless our union."

A Prayer for Protection

Psalm 121 is one of the most eloquent prayers for protection to which parents in the Judaeo-Christian faiths turn.

I look up to the hills,
*   Where will my help come from?*
My help comes from God,
*   Creator of heaven and earth.*

You will not stumble,
*   For your Guardian does not slumber.*
Indeed, the Guardian of Israel
*   neither slumbers nor sleeps.*
God will guard you,
*   God will protect you, close at hand.*
The sun will not strike you by day,
*   The moon will not strike you by night.*
God will guard you against all evil;
*   God will guard you, body and soul.*
God will guard your going out
*   and your coming home, now and forever.*

(Translation by the author)

Victor and Delia, parents of two sons, also pray each day with their children in order to teach them that the universe is safe. "We can trust the cosmos," says Victor. "If there is danger, someone or something in this universe can make it safe enough so that you can get through the night, get through the nightmares, and set them aside. We'll ask the boys to name a blessing they want from God for themselves during that day. Invariably, it's to win in soccer, to get an A on a spelling test."

Physical Illness

Earlier, we met the parents of a four-year-old boy, Jeff, with a kidney disease that has kept him in and out of hospitals all of his short life. In response to their son's physical crises, Kate and Terrance pray. "We started praying, right from the day Jeff was born," Kate says, "because we had no idea what to do. Our minister told us, 'Ask God to help you through, because you can't do it alone.'"

When Kate and Terrance are keeping vigil in intensive care, as they do so often, they will pray, "Lord, please get us through whatever should happen, be it our wishes or not, and that the Lord gives us the strength to cope. Make our son well, take away any pain he might be experiencing, and let your wisdom pour through all the doctors and the nurses who attend to him."

Korean Protective Rituals in Times of Sickness

According to anthropologist Laurel Kendall, Korean village women consult a shaman (called a *mansin*) and hold an exorcism when a child has had a dangerous fever or illness that has lingered despite treatment. Sometimes one exorcism is sufficient to "expel a malevolent ghost or throng of noxious influences." Divination may reveal a "house beset by angry gods and restless ancestors." If this is the case, the family will sponsor a *kut*, "wherein costumed shamans will call down the ancestors and ghosts to feast, play, and make peace with the living family."

Living a Moral Life

Cherie and James senior believe they protect their children through the moral lives they lead. "We try to live a good life and be honest," says Cherie. "If we do that, we believe our prayers for our children and grandchildren will be answered. They're all doing well, so I'd have to say that we're living proof that God protects those who live in his image."

Protective Rituals for a Child's Health in Antigua

In her novel *Annie John*, Jamaica Kincaid describes all the efforts that were made to heal the adolescent, Annie John, suffering from a mysterious illness.

Ma Jolie came. She made cross marks on the soles of my feet, on my knees, on my stomach, in my armpits and on my forehead. She lit two special candles and placed one over the head of my bed and the other near the foot. She said that, with all the rain, it was impossible for anything meaning harm to be living in the yard, so she would not even bother to look there now. She burned incense in one corner of my room. She put a dozen tiny red candles—with white paper on their bottoms, to keep them afloat—in a basin of thick yellow oil. . . . In the basin with the candles she had placed scraps of paper on which were written the names of people who had wanted to harm me. . . . She told my mother, after a careful look around, that there were no spirits in my room or in any other part of the house, and that all the things she did were just a precaution in case anyone should get ideas on hearing that I was in such a weakened condition. . . . She gave my mother some little vials filled with fluids to rub on me. . . . My mother placed them on my shelf, right alongside the bottles of compounds and vitamins and purgatives that Dr. Stephens had prescribed.

Promises

Chakshu Patel, a young Indian woman living in New Jersey, explains that one of the ways her mother, who comes from the state of Gujarat in India, insures protection and good blessings for her children is to make a future promise to make ritual food offerings to the gods or to give a certain amount of money to feed the poor. "One promise my mother has made is that if all of her children graduate from college and find secure jobs, she will make a pilgrimage to a temple in Ahmadabad where she will offer ritual food and money. In Gujarati this is called *prasad theravis*, the promise to make a future offering of food."

Blessings

When Deborah lights candles on Friday evenings to greet the Jewish Sabbath, she holds her hands over her closed eyes a moment longer than is usual. Jews consider the beginning of the Sabbath to be a particularly auspicious time for a parent to act as a conduit for God's blessing. Parents pray that their children lead a life that is faithful to Torah, that they marry, establish a home, and perform good deeds. Many parents will personalize the standard supplication, adding or substituting their own hopes. Deborah, standing with her three children so close by she can smell their newly shampooed hair and freshly laundered Sabbath clothes, focuses on each child. "What I pray," she explains, "is tied into the past week's events: who has been sick, who has been brokenhearted about a gerbil dying or a boy not calling; what's about to happen in the coming week: who has challenges, who will take a new step? For all, I pray: 'Let them be healthy of body and mind. Let them fulfill whatever potential they have; help them fulfill their hopes and dreams. Let them be good and happy, and most important, let them be healthy.'"

When Deborah's husband, Seth, returns home from synagogue later that evening, he holds his hands on each child's head. To his sons, Seth says, "May God make you like Efraim and Menashe." To his daughter, he says, "May God make you like Sarah, Rebecca, Rachel, and Leah." Then, to each child, he says, "May God bless you and protect you. May God illuminate God's countenance for you and be gracious to you. May God turn towards you and give you peace." Seth then

---

A Native American Blessing

This Zuni prayer is spoken at the close of a novice's initiation.

Do not despise the breath of your fathers,
But draw it into your body.
That our roads may reach to where the life-giving road of our
* sun father comes out.*
That, clasping one another tight,
Holding one another fast,
We may finish our roads together;
That this may be, I add to your breath now.
To this end:
May my father bless you with life;
May your road reach to Dawn Lake,
May your road be fulfilled.

---

kisses each child and whispers a few private, silly words. For example, one week his young daughter might hear, "May you have a week of bunnies, unicorns, and rainbows." Seth keeps thinking the children will feel they are too old for the silly endearments, but when he withholds them, their crestfallen looks assure him that the silliness is part of the ritual the children most look forward to.

Worry

Nancie Carmichael, a founding publisher of the magazine *Christian Parenting Today*, considers the protective role worrying plays in a Christian home. She claims that her own prayers sustain her as she worries about her children and attempts to facilitate the process of letting go: "We can't vaccinate our children against the things we worry about as we do with childhood diseases. Our children have their own paths to forge. But at the heart of letting our worries go is this: God will be with our children every moment of the day. . . . The simple reality is that we can only hold our children in our hearts, lift them before God in our prayers, and then trust him completely with them as we let go."

Family therapist Lois Braverman believes that worrying—specifically "active worrying"—can have magical properties. She thinks worrying (and that includes nagging and badgering) indicates a parent's love and might actually ward off misfortune. One of Braverman's clients, a twenty-five-year-old man who had dropped out of graduate school and returned to live with his parents, claimed that his mother was driving him crazy with her worrying. His mother claimed that her capacity for worry was inherited and out of her control. His father could neither constrain his wife from expressing her worries nor restrain his son from exploding at his mother. In time, the household grew more conflictual. After explaining the magical properties of worry to the family, Braverman devised an inventive plan of treatment.

> I instructed the son to call his mother for lunch weekly in order to give her 'active worrying' time as a way to 'protect him.' The son was to hum an old Yiddish song which the father knew and sang when he himself was young and his own mother's worrying got on his nerves. But this humming was

*not to be done in a disrespectful way—rather in a way which
let both the son and the mother know that they were part of a
long, ancient legacy that was much more powerful than just
the two of them. . . . Soon the son went confidently off to
graduate school. . . . The mother continued to worry, but now
in a proud way tied to her history—without shame, apology
or embarrassment.*

Concentration

In her book, *Worlds Beyond My Control*, Jane Lazarre describes
the use of concentration as a protective ritual. When it is close
to her son's two A.M. curfew, and he has not yet returned, she
explains, "I must regress to old forms of magic. I picture him
getting a cab on the street corner, still light and crowded . . .
or he is sitting safely seat-belted in his most reliable friend's
car. . . . I picture him physically to enhance his unarguable
strengths. . . . When it is ten minutes to curfew I invoke the
last-ditch magic of the not-yet-rationally resigned. I picture
him tall, careful, safe. If an image of danger intrudes, I cut it
like an editor trimming a story."

Does Lazarre's ritual work to protect the son? It certainly
works for the mother: She is able to let him go in the first
place and can now make it through until his safe return without calling the police.

Nighttime

Not surprisingly, many protective rituals are linked to nighttime, that frightening threshold through which parents usher
their children with lullabies, songs and stories, and little loving
messages. In bedtime rituals, parents often extend ritual expertise to the child, who helps to determine the songs and stories
as well as the "magic" ordering. In my house, I recall a three-
year-old saying, "We have to start all over again or else I can't
fall asleep. Sing 'Kum Ba Ya' and *then* 'The Itsy Bitsy Spider'!"

Alice D. Roche, my former student, recounts a potent bedtime ritual. "Goodnight felt as if it took hours. My mom crept into my room, lay in bed next to me, and with her thin-edged fingernails, traced circles on my back, as if dragging a feather across my skin. As she did this, she sang 'You are my sunshine, my only sunshine. . . .'" Her voice could melt ice. I would listen to her while I hugged my purring cat and rubbed my security blanket across my mouth. Then we said one "Our Father," prayed for those already in heaven, and God-blessed everyone we could think of.

"After we gave time to God, I'd interrogate my mother. 'Did you have boyfriends before you married Dad?' 'Did anyone else ever tell you he loved you?' 'Were you ever engaged to anyone else?' Then we switched to routine topics: school, family, and friends. I'd keep talking so she'd stay longer and keep scratching my back. Eventually, my father would call up to my mother from his position in front of the TV. 'I'm almost done, Neal,' she'd call down, but she'd stay until I drifted asleep.

"When I started sixth grade, I decided I was too old for our goodnight song and scratches, except for special occasions. When I told my mom, I fought back a surge of tears, but it was decided. Years later, the night before I left for college, my mom came into my room. She sat down on my bed. I didn't want her to feel my fear about leaving home, so I made small talk. Before she got up to leave, she kissed my cheek and started to sing 'You are my sunshine, my only sunshine. . . .' Halfway through, we were both crying too hard for her to finish."

Confidence

Blaise, a twenty-nine-year-old woman who is one of four sisters, believes that she is more independent than most other adults she meets because her Irish Catholic mother routinely projected a sense of confidence and well-being. Says Blaise, "I was never aware that my mother feared anything until I was about ten. By not showing us her fears or worries, we were made to feel secure and safe in whatever we did. My mother made sure we were independent of her, that we could make it on our own and get through in any situation. She always told us that the greatest gift she could give us was independence. She did this by example. A problem arose and she took care of it without ever becoming unhinged. As children, my sisters and I absorbed her confidence, her joy in living, and her enjoyment of new experiences. We felt safe because she regularly told us we had the equipment to succeed in life: intelligence, strong character, and parents who would show us the way. This gave us all an internal sense of security."

This sense of security was put to test when the father of the family died when the sisters were teenagers. Linda, Blaise's older sister explains: "When my father passed away, we moved into public housing, went on welfare and had to use food stamps. It was amazing: Our mom held true to all the outward characteristics she professed when we were small and things were easier. In two years, she went from a retail sales person to management and got us off welfare. She told me the only way I could go to college was if I got a scholarship—and that's what I did. Responsibilities within the family shifted: My oldest sister and I became supervisors, or protectors of the younger girls. We protected the ritual routines of housekeeping and cooking, which really added to our feeling of stability, and we protected our mother's ability to concentrate on her work. We saw the reality: that nothing truly can protect you. But we worked as a unit, we survived the worst situation, and in doing so, fear was eliminated and it freed us to live. I try to instill this belief in my own children: People in tough situations can succeed.

"Today," Blaise says, "when a situation is scary or hectic, I tend to be calm or even laugh about it. My mother did that —she laughed always. I know how to let go of things, even friendships, that are too aggravating or more trouble than they're worth. I feel I can stand up and speak up about my beliefs and feelings. I am almost always willing to take risks. My childhood experience makes me feel excitement about change, new friends, new experiences. I know that I can live anywhere and be home: I have learned that home is where you are comfortable, and if you are comfortable with yourself, then you are home."

Preserving Emotional Confidence in Haitian-American Vodou

Anthropologist Karen Brown, who had befriended a Haitian-American family of Vodou practitioners, noted that the children of the family were always roused when the Vodou spirits would "arrive" in order to "greet them and be blessed by them." As Brown spent more time with this particular family, she also noted that parents practiced "an occasional bit of emotional jouncing." When Maggie's adorable daughter, Betty, came prancing into the room, Maggie would say, "Get away from me! You ugly!" At first, such comments made Brown wince. Eventually, however, Brown understood that this was conscious behavior on Maggie's part, behavior motivated by love and concern. For Maggie, alerting her children to the hardness of life and toughening them up was one of the ways she protected them: "If you push a child off-balance occasionally, that child will learn the inner balance Alourdes [Maggie's mother, a vodou priestess] calls 'confidence in yourself.' "

Fun

Linda, reflecting on the way she attempts to raise her own three little boys today, believes that she makes them feel secure by equipping them with the skills to survive and then getting on with the business of living. Her method: having fun. "I really want to have the best possible time with my children: I plug up the electric outlets, I get the iron out of reach, and we have a great time together. If I spent a ton of time worrying about the culture we lived in, it would be self-centered. We go off to the park, we try to stir up things for the better, working together in the soup kitchen, arranging block parties in our neighborhood. I trust this is what my boys will remember: the way we live together."

Community

"I find comfort in having a sense of community for my children and believe it will give them the protection that an isolated family cannot give," says Tamar Stern, a therapist and mother of three young children. "I try hard to give the children happy experiences with others so they'll have good feelings for people other than our family. Relying on friends and community for support teaches the children that we can't do it all for ourselves. It dilutes the idiosyncratic ways of any one family: The children won't have just us and our fears—they'll have other places and people from which to seek things. In our prayer fellowship, I want them to see religious tradition as something bigger than us, a way of looking outside ourselves for renewal. I want them to be connected to a sacred language of prayer and traditions so that they will speak to them and sustain them, when necessary."

Angels and Elves

"My mother," said Jen, "has always been big on guardian angels. Even now that I'm in college, she gives me a safe feeling when she talks about the guardian angel on my shoulder who watches over me." Victor, the father of two sons, recalls that when he grew up, his mother, an Evangelical Protestant, always said, "There are angels protecting this house." According to Victor, "my mother seemed quite sure that there were real angels, or at least she made them very real for me. She assured us that because of the angels around the house, no one would get us at night, we didn't have to fear the house would burn down." While Victor never saw the angels himself, he thought of them as red flaming beings with wings and swords, just hanging out, ready to defend him.

Delia, Victor's wife, grew up with a Scandinavian grand-mother who believed in elves. "We'd look under the sofa," says Delia, "and she'd describe them to me. She saw them—so I saw them, too. These were protecting elves, elves that helped you do things during the day. Tonight, I told our own sons a story about this family of elves that we've 'had' since he was born. With our own elves, I try to do the same thing my mother did with her elves and my mother-in-law did with her angels—to build in emotional protection."

Amulets

When I speak to her, Delia is holding an enormous silver cross wrapped in gold twine. It hangs on a necklace chain. It's the kind of cross clergy might wear over vestments while of-ficiating, not something anyone would wear daily. "This is the largest cross I have ever bought," Delia explains. "We were shopping at Christmastime, and my older son saw it in a re-ligious bookstore. He sat down, pressed his face on the glass of the counter, and looked at it. I bought two—one for him and one, of course, for his brother. He felt the cross would help him deal with his anxieties in school. He would take the cross to school on certain days of the week when he had stresses coming up. First, he wore it outside his shirt, but when he got to school, I believe he tucked it in. Our own parents would never have allowed us to use religious objects in this way, as if they were rabbits' feet. Elves and angels were ac-ceptable, because they were stories. Physical objects were not encouraged, because in our tradition they were considered su-perstitious. Still, we haven't discouraged our son's use of the cross in this way because it gives him the sense that God is with him, in a warrior sense, fending off evil."

Amulets

In Lebanon, classical protections for children include

blue beads, symbolizing the full moon, the "giver of life";

horseshoe charms, representing the crescent moon, a symbol of power and good fortune;

the Hand of Fatima, made of blue glass, wood, silver, or gold, symbolizing the hand of the dead that plucks out the evil eye and blinds it; and

glass eyes. This black pupil surrounded by blue repels the evil eye through imitative magic, like repelling like.

My Own Ritual Responses

While considering if I, myself, was ever protected by amulets, I find myself fingering the two pieces of jewelry I always wear: my mother's red Victorian glass ring and an eyelike locket, with a diamond chip in the center of a white circle surrounded by a blue rim, that hangs on a neck chain. The initials of my mother's maiden name are etched, in incorrect order, on the gold back of the locket. She was given the locket at birth, by a relative who had gotten her name a little wrong. The ring was a present she received in childhood from her Aunt Rose. My mother had given both the ring and necklace to me as a child. Receiving them made me feel valued, mature, responsible, and linked to my mother and her childhood. While I was never conscious that the red of the ring was the red that warded off evil or that the eye shape of the locket served the same symbolic purpose, I hardly took either off. I suppose I was subliminally aware that both served as amulets, signs that my mother's protective wish accompanied me everywhere. Then it strikes me, and the feeling is so spooky: On the day of my car accident that had set off my overprotection,

I wore neither the ring nor the locket—I had taken them off the night before and replaced them with dressier jewelry to wear to a party. On the day of my accident, the ring and the locket lay on my dresser—I had forgotten to put them back on.

I won't say I get a full-fledged "Twilight Zone" feeling as I consider the uncanny connection between the accident and the absent amulets, but it does make me recall ways in which my sister Susan and I were protected from imaginary, as well as real, dangers. In particular, our mother feared the evil eye. This was the catch-all term she used to decribe the evil wishes of jealous people. We could not walk out the front door of our house without having our shoes pulled away from our heels or having our collars or skirtbands stretched back so our mother could drop down a piece of red string. Red would protect us from the malevolence disguised in the compliments we would garner for our new velveteen dresses, my singing voice, Susan's piano playing, or our apparent good health. These compliments we received, she warned us, were the disguised evil wishes of jealous people. Unlike some children who find their parents' protective practices charming or, at least, tolerable, this stuff annoyed me. It was so Old World, so cockeyed. As soon as I was out of my mother's sight, I always pulled the red strings away from my body and threw them out the window or under a bush.

In retrospect, I realize that if not for the "protection" of my mother's red string, she would not have given us her blessings to go places or do things. Providing a red string was no tiny gesture to appease evil spirits. This calmed my mother's fears long enough to let us out of her sight for short spells. It was a concrete, sanctioned measure her culture provided to contain terrors.

After my own period of overprotectiveness toward my children had gone on for several months, I was already gaining better cognitive control over the situation. I knew I still needed to turn to a ritual that acknowledged the evil that had been unleashed, as well as my own terror and the vulnerability of my children. To begin to give closure to this long and difficult episode, I turned to a playful variation on my mother's evil-eye precautions.

I brought candles and cinnamon sticks to my friend Charlotte's house and sat out back by her swimming pool. Half silly, half serious, we made a little pyre and burned the spice, scattering the ashes in the water and on the ground. It was all an improvisation, a take-off on a ceremony that marks the separation between the sacred time and space of the Sabbath day and the six profane days of the week. Among its ritual symbols are fire and spice. Digging the last cinnamon ashes into Charlotte's floral border, I announced that this ritual would be a marker in time, separating a time of endangerment from a time, I wished, of greater safety. "Let the evil be gone," we said, and, twisting our heads over our shoulders, we made the spitting sounds our mothers and grandmothers used to make to ward off evil: "ptu, ptu, ptu," over and over again.

Of course, I never believed for a moment that an offering of burnt cinnamon would protect my children. I did believe, however, that I needed to give ceremony to my fears: In naming them, particularly in the presence of Charlotte, who had been in the accident with me, I could begin to relinquish them. Confronting my terror, talking about it aloud, even joking about it self-mockingly, served to dilute it. Curiously, as each day passed, the terror abated and I was able to give my children more freedom. And with that ceremony, I continued the process of confronting just how much fear I still held. Only when I began to focus on the daily ceremonies of protection—the prayers, blessings, goodnights, and good-byes that are part of our ritual regime—was I able to relinquish the extreme over-protection and protect, as I had hoped, adequately.

Taking Stock

What are the protective rituals that you are already aware of performing?

Which would you classify as religious, in a conventional sense? Which would you say are not religious but are important, repeated acts?

If you, yourself, don't perform any such rituals, what are some of the protective rituals performed in your religious tradition or ancestral culture. Dig deeply into your own background and investigate the ways your ancestors dealt with their fears of real and imagined dangers through the means of amulets for pregnancy and childbirth, newborn-baby ceremonies, naming ceremonies, puberty or coming-of-age rituals, charms and exorcisms for mental and physical illness.

What personal, made-up protective rituals do you perform regularly, from time to time, or spontaneously as the need appears?

What songs, music, stories, or poems give you and your children a feeling of being safe? What comforting foods do you prepare for yourself or your children when someone feels ill or anxious?

Perhaps you are performing protective rituals unconsciously: Take note of what you do each morning as the kids leave for school. While some of the words you say and actions you perform may seem to have only a material function, the repetition and predictability make them into a kind of ritual with its own liturgy and gestures. "Did you pack your lunch?" "Wear your blue coat." "Remember to look before you cross." "Give me a kiss good-bye. (Mwa!) See you later, have a good day." What similar ceremonies are in your family's repertoire?

Consider your nighttime routine, which may hold all the elements of a protective ritual. How have the bedtime rituals —the songs, stories, and kisses—changed as your children have grown older? Can you recall who initiated the changes or

---

What kind of rituals do you remember your parents performing for your safety?

At a workshop on rituals of protection, one woman recalled that when her first baby was born, her mother-in-law called from Barbados to remind her to open a Bible to the 23rd Psalm and place it in the upper-right corner of her daughter's crib. On the Bible, she was to lay a pair of scissors, opened and pointed upward, in order to keep away evil. The Bible and scissors were to stay in place until the baby was confirmed at three months of age.

One man recalled that his father would tell him that he'd have good luck if he said the word "rabbit" upon waking up and getting out of bed on the first day of each month.

Another man recalled that whenever he or his siblings moved to someplace new—at first to college dorms, then to apartments here and there—their mother would bring or send a piece of coal and some salt. The coal and salt symbolized her wish that their homes have warmth and their lives have flavor.

---

how each component got there in the first place? When your child has a nightmare, what are some of the ways you have reacted?

What about rituals that are clearly not religious but have a sacred feel to them: like wishing on the candles of a birthday cake; breaking a wishbone; finding an eyelash on someone's face, placing it on your finger tip, and saying, "Make a wish"? What wishes and hopes do you have for your children? How are you aware of articulating those wishes?

Take note, as well, of the ritualized way in which you may inadvertantly be teaching your children that they cannot protect themselves. Often, the litanies we recite of the bad things

Protective Rituals in Contemporary American Culture

- Keeping a baby book
- Telling stories of sandmen and guardian angels
- Singing lullabies
- Knitting sweaters, booties, and crib blankets
- Making limited preparations for a new baby
- Making elaborate preparations for a new baby
- Checking on children at night after they're asleep and rearranging their covers
- Keeping a child's picture displayed at home, at the office, or in a wallet
- Encouraging a child to bond with a blanket or stuffed animal
- Sending care packages of food to camp and college; writing letters and postcards, even daily
- Calling out the same warnings, day after day: "Look both ways," "Buckle up," "Put your button down," "Remember to button up," "Wear your hat," "Don't stay out too late," "Call when you get there"
- Purchasing protective apparatuses that fill both physical and psychic needs: intercoms for baby's room, life preservers, bicycle helmets, protective equipment for sports, first-aid kits, smoke alarms, fire extinguishers, fire ladders
- Serving a hot breakfast; packing a wholesome school lunch
- Having set times for family dinners
- Regular phone calls to latchkey children and to grown children living away from home
- Saving money or buying savings bonds for a child's future or education
- Naming a child's legal guardians or godparents
- Making a vow, such as "If my child recovers, I'll give up smoking!"
- Making the world a better place for all children:
    - Protecting the environment
    - Working for peace and social justice
    - Protesting nuclear plants
    - Going to rallies and meetings; making phone calls
    - Wearing buttons for special causes
    - Writing letters and telegrams to elected officials
    - Signing petitions

that can befall our children serve to make them more fearful than careful. This letter, written by Emily Dickinson to Thomas Wentworth Higginson in August 1862 describes the fears that were regularly communicated to Dickinson but, mercifully, did not take hold.

> *When much in the Woods as a little Girl, I was told that the Snake would bite me, that I might pick a poisonous flower, or Goblins kidnap me, but I went on and met no one but Angels, who were far shyer of me than I could be of them, so I haven't that confidence in fraud which many exercise.*

We might pay attention to the phrases we regularly repeat to our own children that are meant to be encouraging but end up teaching and reinforcing fear, such as "Don't worry about that dog. He won't bite you."

Parting Thoughts

As I conclude, I cannot be less than absolutely honest here: Beyond all the rational parenting, beyond all the rituals, I continue to carry fear around with me—fear that something awful will happen to my children. Inside, I am aware that a potential overprotector still lurks. It does go with the territory. As author Ron Carlson writes, parenthood is "a mission that demands we protect our children and all too often leaves us powerless to do so." In a certain mood, if a child is away from home, I can still lie anxiously in bed, awaiting the phone call that announces a sick child, a hurt child, a child jolted by violence. I still imagine situations in which I, as the parent, could have been more vigilant—if only I had anticipated, if only I had thought, if only I had been less trusting, less cavalier.

I cannot forget the night my daughter's principal never arrived at a committee meeting. The vice-principal, speaking in hushed tones, announced that the principal wasn't coming because he had gotten a call from his son's high-school office.

A soccer accident, the vice-principal whispered. Rushed to the emergency ward. Surgery to save his spleen. Critical condition, intensive care. We parents and teachers sitting around a table stared down at our hearts, took large deep breaths in through our mouths, stiffened up. We shook our head, "no."

"I thought soccer was a safe sport," said a mother whose son played on the same team.

"No sport is safe," said a father.

I thought, None of our children is safe.

I still don't take either of my daughters' well-being for granted, and I'm sure I never will. Each time they return from school and I hear them, from my upstairs office, push the front door open and call, "He-lo-oh, we're back," I feel relief, then gratitude. I shouldn't overstate this: It's not as though they've returned from fighting in the Persian Gulf War or reentered Earth's atmosphere. Going to school by bus is not one of life's high-stake operations, and I know that. I suppose my feeling of gratitude is akin to the feeling I have when I open the mailbox and get good mail, open up the fridge and see there's still food left: a sense that the world is working as it should be if we're fortunate. I feel lucky when the girls return safely. When they are late, and I feel myself entering into a state of panic, the world draining of all its color, I give myself the calming pep talks that have, by now, become a ritual for me: "Substitute drivers get lost, buses start late and break down. Whatever the problem is, it is probably no big deal; whatever it is, we will be able to handle it or get help."

When terror and pessimism overwhelm us, and pep talks won't do the trick, we all need to use whatever means we can to move beyond our fears, challenge our urges to overprotect, whatever their source, and let our children still know freedom. As Phyllis Theroux has written: "We do not easily send our children into the darkness. But it seems to be the only way to the light."

If that means we have no choice but to change the world

to increase the available light, then that, perhaps, is what we ought to do. These, perhaps, are the ultimate protective rituals: the ethical and political acts we perform to make the world less violent, less toxic, less harrowing, less meager in its resources, and more conducive to the flourishing of all children everywhere. Perform these rituals of repair—perform them with your children and for them.

Notes

Preface

P. xiv ["living arrows are set forth . . ."] Khalil Gibran, *The Prophet* (New York: Knopf, 1923), 18.

Chapter One

P. 3 ["The experiencing of frustrations . . ."] D. W. Winnicott, "A Note on Normality and Anxiety" in *Collected Papers: Through Paediatrics to Psycho-Analysis* (London: Tavistock, 1958), 4.

P. 5 ["undue or excessive protection . . ."] Webster's Third International Dictionary (Springfield, Mass.: G. C. Merriam Co., 1971).

P. 5 [the term *momism* . . .] Philip Wylie, *Generation of Vipers* (New York: Holt, Rinehart, and Winston, 1942), 208.

P. 5 [In 1943 psychiatrist D. M. Levy . . .] D. M. Levy, *Maternal Overprotection*, 2nd ed. (New York: Norton, 1966). Republished in part as "The Concept of Maternal Protection" in *Parenthood: It's Psychology and Psychopathology*, edited by E. James Anthony and Therese Benedek (Boston: Little, Brown and Company, 1970), 387–409.

P. 7 ["mother-daughter relationships . . ."] Nancy Chodorow, *The Reproduction of Mothering: Psychoanalysis and the Sociology of Gender* (Berkeley: University of California Press, 1978), 213.

P. 7 [For Dr. Rubin, overprotected children . . .] Theodore Isaac Rubin, *Child Potential* (New York: Continuum, 1990), 106–109.

Chapter Two

P. 15 [Margaret Mead could write a government pamphlet . . .] Margaret Mead, *A Creative Life for Your Children* (United States Department of Health, Education and Welfare, Children's Bureau, 1962), 34–35.

P. 16 ["When I was growing up, parents and children harbored . . ."] Jackie Leo, *Family Circle* (March 12, 1994), 95.

P. 17 [the bloody flux . . .] Mary Cable, *The Little Darlings* (New York: Charles Scribner's Sons, 1975), 142.

P. 19 ["because of its nightmare quality . . ."] "California Town Mourns Abducted Girl," Jane Gross, *The New York Times* (December 6, 1993).

P. 20 [Though violent crime in general has leveled off since 1990 . . .] Isabel Wilkerson, "Two Boys, a Debt, a Gun, a Victim," *The New York Times* (May 16, 1994), A1, A14.

P. 21 [According to a 1989 Justice Department survey . . .] William Celic, "Suburban and Rural Schools Learning that Violence Isn't Confined to the Cities," *The New York Times* (April 21, 1993), B11.

P. 23 [According to health experts . . .] Nancy Gibbs, "How Should We Teach Our Children About Sex?" *Time* (May 24, 1993), 51.

P. 25 [phenol, an ingredient in furniture and floor polish . . .] Debra Lynn Dadd, *The Nontoxic Home and Office* (Los Angeles: Jeremy P. Tarcher, Inc., 1992).

P. 27 [Abduction, according to journalist Noelle Oxenhandler . . .] Noelle Oxenhandler, "Polly's Face" *The New Yorker* (November 29, 1993), 95.

P. 28 [It is sad . . .] Elizabeth Crow, *The New York Times Book Review* (June 20, 1993), 25.

P. 28 ["It is this very act of overprotectiveness . . ."] Karla Hull, *Safe Passages: A Guide for Teaching Children Personal Safety* (San Diego: Dawn Sign Press, 1986), 17.

Chapter Three

P. 40 [IQ scores tend to be lower . . .] Arnold Sameroff, Ronald Siefer, Ralph Barocas, Melvin Zax and Greenspan. "Intelligence Quotient Scores of 4-Year-Old Children: Social-Environmental Risk Factors" in *Pediatrics* 79 (1987), 343–350.

P. 42 [Numerous factors predict a child's resilience.] James Garbarino, Nancy Dubrow, Kathleen Kostelny and Carole Pardo. *Children in Danger: Coping with the Consequences of Community Violence* (San Francisco: Jossey-Bass, 1992), 100–114.

P. 46 ["caregivers who were overprotected during childhood are likely to view the world . . ."] Deborah B. Jacobvitz, Elizabeth Morgan, Molly D. Kretchman, and Yvonne Morgan, "The Transmission of Mother-Child

Boundary Disturbances Across Three Generations" in *Development and Psychology* 3 (1991), 516.

Chapter Five

P. 76 [" 'I couldn't stand watching them grow up . . .' "] John Irving, *The World According to Garp* (New York: Pocket, 1976), 604.

P. 76 ["Our children are vulnerable, so we are vulnerable in them."] Stephen Langfur, *Confessions from a Jericho Jail* (New York: Grove Weidenfeld, 1992), 253.

P. 83 ["an initial tap may prove unsuccessful."] Elizabeth Kristol, "Picture Perfect: The Politics of Prenatal Testing" in *First Things* 32 (April 1993), 17–24.

P. 85 ["souped up on adrenaline."] Perri Klass, *Baby Doctor* (New York: Random House, 1992), 12.

P. 92 ["Feeling deeply anxious is often a result of feeling fearful . . ."] Michael Waldholtz, "Panic Pathway" in *Wall Street Journal* (September 29, 1993), A12.

P. 95 ["who makes active adaptation to the infant's needs . . ."] D. W. Winnicott, *Playing and Reality* (New York: Basic, 1971), 10.

P. 95 ["gradual failing of adaptation . . ."] D. W. Winnicott, *The Maturational Process and the Facilitating Environment* (New York: International University Press, 1965), 86–87.

P. 95 ["intrusive caregiving patterns during the first year of life increase children's vulnerability . . ."] Deborah B. Jacobvitz, Elizabeth Morgan, Molly D. Kretchman, and Yvonne Morgan, "The Transmission of Mother-Child Boundary Disturbances Across Three Generations" in *Development and Psychology* 3 (1991), 514.

Chapter Six

P. 103 ["are typically easily frustrated by problem-solving tasks."] Deborah B. Jacobvitz, Elizabeth Morgan, Molly D. Kretchman, and Yvonne Morgan, "The Transmission of Mother-Child Boundary Disturbances Across Three Generations" in *Development and Psychology* 3 (1991), 514.

P. 104 [When their children are distressed, caregivers who are preoccupied with their own unmet needs . . .] ibid, 514.

Chapter Eight

P. 147 ["She no longer had any power . . ."] Robb Forman Dew, *Fortunate Lives* (New York: William Morrow, 1992), 137.

P. 151 [In a study of 150 undergraduates . . .] Mark Whisman and Paul Kwon, "Parental Representations, Cognitive Distortions, and Mild Depression" in *Cognitive Therapy and Research*, volume 16 (October 1992), 557–568.

P. 152 ["She always said, 'You can do whatever you set your mind to do.'"] Bernard Weintraub, "How Orlando Finds Her True Self," *New York Times* (February 15, 1993), C14.

P. 159 ["We children always knew what you were doing with our goldfish . . ."] Marcia Ann Hain, *No Mommies at Millbrook* (self-published, 1989), 25.

P. 168 [in a study of adolescents with chronic disabilities . . .] Robert W. Blum, "Chronic Illness and Disability in Adolescence," *Journal of Adolescent Health*, volume 13 (July 1992), 364–368.

Chapter Nine

P. 177 ["We are never so defenseless against suffering . . ."] Sigmund Freud, *Civilization and Its Discontents* (New York: Norton, 1930), 33.

P. 178 ["took a charm from around his neck."] Laurence Yep, *The Rainbow People* (New York: Harper and Row, 1989), 87.

P. 179 ["a female figure holding children in the security of her lap."] Ross Kraemer, *Her Share of the Blessings: Women's Religions among Pagans, Jews, and Christians in the Greco-Roman World* (New York and Oxford: Oxford University Press, 1992), 62.

P. 179 [Infants and children in ancient Greece and Rome were considered especially susceptible . . .] Eugene S. McCartney, "Praise and Dispraise in Folklore" in *The Evil Eye: A Folklore Casebook*, Alan Dundes, ed. (New York and London: Garland, 1981), 12.

P. 179 ["If you kiss your child . . ."] ibid, 12.

P. 179 [In Greece, in the early 1800s . . .] ibid, 14.

P. 182 ["Whenever we are overwhelmed by natural events . . ."] Neil Gilman, *Sacred Fragments* (Philadelphia: Jewish Publication Society, 1990), 219.

P. 183 ["We get out the powerful magic of our people . . ."] Vanessa L. Ochs, Letters to the Editor, *Tikkun* (March/April 1991).

P. 184 ["We know our love is not powerful enough to protect them from all harm . . ."] Ann and Barry Ulanov, *Primary Speech: A Psychology of Prayer* (Atlanta: John Knox Press, 1982), 86.

P. 186 ["assume that primitive man had great confidence in his wishes."] Sigmund Freud, *Totem and Taboo* (New York: Vintage, 1918), 109.

P. 187 ["To speak of ritual is not necessarily to speak of religion."] Tom F. Driver, *The Magic of Ritual* (San Francisco: Harper Collins, 1992), 5.

P. 187 ["Though people today seldom dress in a frightening costume . . ."] James H. S. Bossard and Eleanor S. Boll, *Ritual in Family Living* (Philadelphia: University of Pennsylvania Press, 1950), 22–23.

P. 190 ["There exists an instinctual desire to put some kind of stamp . . ."] Anne Carson, *Spiritual Parenting in the New Age* (Freedom, Calif.: The Crossing Press, 1989), 92, 94–95.

P. 193 ["expell a malevolent ghost or throng of noxious influences . . ."] Laurel Kendall, *Shamans, Housewives and Other Restless Spirits: Women in Korean Ritual Life* (Honolulu: University of Hawaii Press, 1987), 89.

P. 194 ["Ma Jolie came . . ."] Jamaica Kincaid, *Annie John* (New York: Farrar, Straus and Giroux, 1985), 116–117.

P. 196 ["Do not despise the breath . . ."] *World Scripture: A Comparative Anthology of Sacred Texts* (New York: Paragon House, 1991), 170.

P. 197 ["We can't vaccinate our children against the things we worry about . . ."] Nancie Carmichael, *Christian Parenting Today* (September/October 1993), 47.

P. 197 ["I instructed the son to call his mother for lunch weekly . . ."] Lois Braverman, "The Magical Properties of Worrying," *Lilith* (Spring 1992), 32–31.

P. 198 ["I must regress to old forms of magic."] Jane Lazarre, *Worlds Beyond My Control* (New York: Dutton, 1991), 162.

P. 201 ["Get away from me! You ugly!"] Karen Brown, *Mama Lola: a Vodou Priestess in Brooklyn* (Berkeley: University of California Press, 1991), 373.

P. 204 [In Lebanon, classical protections for children include . . .] Jamal Karam Harfouche, "The Evil Eye and Infant Health in Lebanon" in *The Evil Eye: A Folklore Casebook*, Alan Dundes, ed. (New York: Garland, 1981), 95.

P. 210 ["When much in the Woods as a little Girl . . ."] Richard Sewall, *The Life of Emily Dickinson* (New York: Farrar, Straus and Giroux, 1974), 559–60.

P. 210 ["a mission that demands we protect our children and all too often leaves us powerless to do so."] Ron Carlson in a review of *Fortunate Lives* by Robb Rorman Dew, *New York Times Book Review* (March 22, 1992), 10.

P. 211 ["We do not easily send our children into the darkness . . ."] Phyllis Theroux, *Night Lights: Bedtime Stories for Parents in the Dark* (New York: Viking, 1987), 179.